the Hermitage
Treasures of World Art

the Hermitage
Treasures of World Art

WITH TEXT BY

Oleg Yakovlevich Neverov and
Dmitry Pavlovich Alexinsky

arca publishers

BEAUX
ARTS
EDITIONS

PP. 2

Rembrandt Harmensz. van Rijn. *Portrait of an Old Man in Red.* First half of the 1650s. Oil on canvas.
42 ½ x 33 ⅞ in. (108 x 86 cm).
In the 1650s Rembrandt produced a series of superb portraits that were not directly commissioned, and so the names of those depicted remain unknown. This work's conventional title stresses the importance of the main color. Here the artist uses his favorite combination of red with brown ochre, in gradations from darkest to almost white. The sense of the greatness of an ordinary person is intensified by his pose and the color of his clothing, which call to mind portraits of popes and cardinals.

PP. 6

Anthony van Dyck. *Portrait of the Sisters Elizabeth and Philadelphia Wharton.* 1640. Oil on canvas.
63 ¾ x 51 ⅛ in. (162 × 130 cm).
Van Dyck painted the daughters of Lord Philip Wharton, a prominent English politician of the Civil War period and close supporter of Oliver Cromwell, for his family gallery on the Winchendon estate. The girls, four and five years old, pose in their smart dresses like real ladies of the court. The strange leaning tree in the background may be an allusion to their mother, Lord Wharton's first wife, Elizabeth Wandesford, who died shortly before the portrait was made.

Beaux Arts Editions
Published by Rizzoli International Publications, Inc.
300 Park Avenue South
New York, NY 10010
www.rizzoliusa.com

Published in coordination with
ARCA Publishers
43 Moika Emb.
St. Petersburg, 191065, Russia

Project coordination: Olga Borodyanskaya
Managing Russian editor: Alexei Shestakov
Translation from Russian: Paul Williams
Translation editor: Nina Zhutovsky
Contributing Editor/Picture Research: Polina Yermakova
Scanning and color correction: Igor Bondar
Photography: Leonard Heifetz, Yury Molodkovets, Vladimir Terebenin, Valery Zubarov, and Victor Savik

Project editor: Melissa P. Veronesi
Editor: Mary Ellen Wilson
Book design by Ziga Design, LLC: Charles J. Ziga, Veronica Naranjo, and James F. Kahnweiler

Printed in China

ISBN-13: 978-0-88363-470-7

Acknowledgments

Rizzoli would like to thank the following people who were instrumental in assembling these volumes. Over the past four years, the teams from Russia and the United States have strived to put together a two-volume set that showcases the beauty and majesty of the State Hermitage Museum. We would like to thank Hugh Levin, for the conception of this spectacular series of art books; Olga Borodyanskaya, for her incredible leadership and dedication; Mary Ellen Wilson, for her diligent work and guidance with the structure of these two volumes; Alexei Shestakov, for his editorial eye and patience through the dozens of revisions; Polina Yermakova, for her iconographic research and enormous help in procuring all high-quality images for reproduction; and all of the ARCA team members for their hard work in producing these beautiful volumes on the State Hermitage. We would also like to express our deep gratitude and thanks to Dr. Mikhail Piotrovsky, Director of the Hermitage, for his invaluable support.

The publisher would also like to thank Charles Ziga and Ziga Design for their support and organization in keeping these two volumes in order and also Debby Zindell for her careful proofreader's eye. Special thanks to Rizzoli's publisher, Charles Miers, for pushing these books to stand as a symbol of excellence in the wide field of art book publications.

ARCA publishers, who prepared this project in Russia, express their gratitude to Professor Sergei Daniel, who played a decisive role in shaping the concept for the two-volume set and to a large extent defined its overall structure. The Russian editor would like to thank the entire Rizzoli team for their invariable patience and understanding, and in particular Melissa Veronesi, through whose constant contact all the problems involved in bringing the project to press were successfully resolved. My particular thanks to my American colleague Mary Ellen Wilson; to the Russian-English translator, Paul Williams, who made a large number of valuable clarifications; and also to Irina Shestakova, Polina Yermakova, Katya Vassilyeva and Andrei Naslednikov in Saint Petersburg and Anna Medyantseva in New York, whose advice and opinions gave me great support.

Contents

The Hermitage
Is Exceptional

The Hermitage—yesterday's Imperial, today's State—is one of the world's foremost museums. Such museums are no longer made and probably never will be.

Its peculiarities, scale, and depth arise from a long and complex history, from the empire with its pride and desire to admire the works of various cultures. A dialogue of cultures is the meaning and aim of any museum but is especially important for such universal, encyclopedic museums as the Hermitage. It presents different world cultures, not just art, relating and comparing them. Encyclopedic museums are a special historical type that came before national, regional, and local ones. They were, from the outset, intended not for idle tourists but for visitors eager to know the world, to grasp its complexity and perceive the beauty and pleasure revealed by differences in civilizations, cultures, aesthetics, and artistic schools.

The Hermitage is an illustrious, glorious name that for people around the world conjures up an image of wealth, beauty, variety, traditions, and new impressions. A few other museums are akin to the Hermitage in their fundamentally encyclopedic nature, the range and diversity of their collections, their symbolic meaning for humanity. Such "fellows," with which the Hermitage constantly coordinates policy, are the Louvre, the British Museum (and National Gallery), the Metropolitan Museum, and the museum complex in Berlin. This special league is united by typological kinship, common traditions and ambitions, and research experience.

The Hermitage is an encyclopedic museum, but this encyclopedia is written in Russian, a product of the efforts and tastes of Russian collectors. It reflected the history of Russian culture, its adoption of old and new traditions from Europe, a Russian understanding and interpretation of European and world culture. The Hermitage's great collections, besides all else, mirror the formation of Russian culture in open dialogue with others. The Hermitage's famous Rembrandts are Russian Rembrandts that for centuries have educated Russian eyes and tastes; they are a reminder of the enlightened Catherine the Great, who opportunely acquired such amazing masterpieces. The Hermitage's Matisses are a part of Russian cultural history. The Russian avant-garde grew up on them and they are a monument to the great Muscovite collectors who opportunely recognized some of the greatest artists of the dawning twentieth century. The astonishing collections of Scythian gold and Greek artifacts from the Black Sea coast are Russia's prehistory, with its combination of the nomadic and classical, the Asian and European legacies.

The Hermitage collections were assembled by Russian nobles, travelers, archaeologists, and businessmen. Studied by Russian scholars and presented by them to the world, they have become part of the common cultural heritage. The creators and researchers of these collections form a roll-call of glorious names in Russian history and culture. Monarchs, aristocrats, art patrons and merchants, historians and archaeologists—Peter I, Catherine II, the Stroganovs, Shchukins and Morozovs, Kushelev-Bezborodko, Gedeonov, Orbeli, Artamonov, Levinson-Lessing, Boris Piotrovsky, Griaznov, Lukonin, Vladislav Glinka—they all left part of their souls in the Hermitage, and the museum remembers.

The Hermitage is one among the great museums, but a number of features make it exceptional. It is not just a monument of world and Russian culture, but also a monument of Russian statehood. The museum always existed alongside the chief imperial residence, and now the Winter Palace is part of it. This was the setting for key events in Russian history; the memory of them lives on and is part of the story the museum tells, directly or indirectly. Here Peter the Great lived and died, Catherine II gathered her friends, Alexander II expired after the terrorist bomb, and Nicholas II grieved over "Bloody Sunday." Here the first Russian parliament was opened and the country's tragic entry into the First World War was declared. Here the Provisional Government was deposed and the Socialist revolution came about. Here, during the siege of Leningrad, culture stood up to world-ranking evil. The Hermitage complex is a symbol of

Russia's greatest victories over foreign aggression. It is a symbol of the preservation of Russian and world cultural heritage in the hardest of times.

The Hermitage is a wonderful encyclopedia of architecture. In its buildings the European traditions of the Baroque, Classicism, and Historicism receive a Russian interpretation, resulting in masterpieces that adorn our beautiful city. Rastrelli, Rossi, Quarenghi, Klenze, and Stasov are names with a place in both Russian and European architectural histories. They created the unique ensemble in central St. Petersburg, the heart of which is today's Hermitage. Its magnificent structures are set off by two great spaces: the Neva and Palace Square. The views through the windows and the museum's interiors merge into a unique visual symphony.

The Hermitage has come to symbolize Russia's own political and cultural history and, at the same time, its involvement in European culture. The French name sounds quite natural to the Russian ear—one of the manifestations of the "universal sympathy" of the Russian soul and Russian culture that characterized our country long before Dostoyevsky pointed it out.

The Hermitage is a living, dynamic museum. Throughout its almost 250-year history, it has not just developed, it has transformed space—cultural, architectural, urban, virtual. The museum grew up next to the palace and subordinated it to its displays, extending in a neat line along the river. In the twentieth century it "embraced" Palace Square, making it a part of the museum space, uniting it with the mighty Neva and the lesser rivers and canals. The palatial spaces merged with the museum; historical interiors next to picture galleries. Old and new art in constant dialogue. The Winter Palace, the Small, Old, and New Hermitages, the Hermitage Theater, and the General Staff building, with the famous arch and Alexander Column, are becoming the core of a new "Greater Hermitage" that encompasses branches such as the Menshikov Palace and the Porcelain Factory Museum. The newly completed Open Repository in the Staraya Derevnia district provides, for the first time, the ideal conditions for storage and preservation. It also solves the perpetual problem of providing access to the museum's immense stocks. The complex is open to visitors, who are able to view items presented "storeroom-style"— a wholly new impression.

The Hermitage is at the center of further "concentric circles." Next comes the circle of our many exhibitions outside St. Petersburg. The Hermitage is a generous museum, willing to share its treasures in return for respect for its great collections. The following circle is made up of Hermitage satellites in Amsterdam, Kazan, London, Ferrara, and Vyborg. In them, the museum arranges exhibitions, organizes research and restoration, lectures and work with children, plans and operates joint events. And then comes the Internet, a virtual presence around the globe. The Hermitage Web site is also our pride and innovation. A virtual panoramic museum, digital collection, online academy, discussion club, ingenious systems for seeking analogies, and much more, all serve the chief task of using the Hermitage to transform the cultural space—from the architectural to the political to the virtual—to make the museum's collections as accessible as possible to the world at large.

The Hermitage's dynamic development is a constantly renewed tradition that, over the centuries, has protected it from all manner of misfortunes. Our museum has experienced attacks and mortal threats like none other. Three times it has been evacuated: during Napoleon's invasion, in the First World War, and before the siege of Leningrad. On the last occasion, the museum's very existence was in jeopardy, had the Nazis prevailed. The collections have been successfully defended as well, during the terrible fire of 1837, the storming of the Winter Palace in 1917, and the repressions of 1937. Immense harm was caused in Soviet times by the transfer of works to museums in Moscow and elsewhere and by the sale of others abroad. The collections were also under threat from ideological restrictions. The return to capitalism brought new, legal challenges to the integrity and accessibility of the stocks. We had to resist commercialization and new sales, privatization and "corporate raiders," the claims of the "home" countries of many traditional collections and the actions of the descendants of historical owners and users of cultural objects.

The Hermitage responded to all these challenges with dynamic expansion and increased activity. When some collections were removed, we managed to add others. The museum lacked funds for purchases but was enriched by vigorous archaeological activities. Friends of the museum never stopped sharing parts of their collections with it. For all problems we invariably found a solution that ultimately left the museum a winner.

The struggle for culture is an inseparable component of the intellectual education of society. The Hermitage strongly champions the retention of certain privileges for cultural institutions and seeks to make clear to the authorities and the public the exceptional significance of museums as guardians of our cultural heritage—the national memory and the national idea.

The Hermitage belongs *urbi et orbi*—"to the city and the world"—and toward them its activities have been directed for well over two centuries.

—Mikhail Piotrovsky
Director of the State Hermitage

The Hermitage
Treasures of World Art

OPPOSITE
*The Peter the Great Hall
(Small Throne Room) in the
Winter Palace. Architect:
Auguste Ricard de
Montferrand, 1833; restored
1837–39 (after the fire)
under the direction of
Vasily Stasov.
This memorial hall,
dedicated to the first Russian
emperor and founder of St.
Petersburg, was created on
the initiative of Nicholas I.
The sumptuous Empire-style
decor incorporates attributes
of the great monarch: his
Latin monogram (crossed
Ps), double-headed eagles,
and crowns. The
monumental niche contains
an allegorical depiction of
Peter with the goddess
Minerva, painted by the
Venetian artist Jacopo
Amiconi (1730s), and a
gilded silver throne made in
London in the same period
by Nicholas Klausen.*

The State Hermitage in St. Petersburg is among the premier European museums housed in palatial residences, just as the Louvre is in Paris, the Palazzo Pitti in Florence, and the Vatican Palace in Rome. Like these illustrious institutions, the Hermitage is infused with the spirit of history: it stands as a monument to the Enlightenment culture that shaped it and embodies a symbol of Russia's rich past. Throughout nearly one and a half centuries, it evolved gradually from a private court institution into a vast public museum encompassing five buildings and more than three million artifacts. The extremely rich collections gathered within, as well as the facades and interiors of the structures themselves, reflect not only changes in aesthetic thinking and artistic fashion in the eighteenth and nineteenth centuries, but also the personal tastes of the imperial collectors who succeeded one another as stewards of this treasury of world art.

Although Catherine the Great (r. 1762–96) is justly regarded as the founder of the Hermitage, the tremendous architectural ensemble that now forms the museum complex was in fact begun by her predecessor, Empress Elizabeth (r. 1741–62). It was on Elizabeth's instructions that, in 1752, the Italian architect Francesco Bartolomeo Rastrelli (1700–1771) set about designing a new urban imperial residence, the present Winter Palace, on the bank of the river Neva. The previous palaces that had existed on the site did not satisfy the ambitions of the daughter of Peter the Great, during whose reign the Russian Empire had claimed its right to a prominent role in European politics. Empress Elizabeth required a sumptuous and impressive residence that would reflect the glorious achievements of her own rule and provide a worthy setting for the brilliance of her court. The new palace was constructed, in the words of its creator, "for the sole glory of all Russia."

Rastrelli, the son of a Russified Italian sculptor, had come to St. Petersburg in 1716 with his father, who had been invited to enter the service of the Russian court. By midcentury the younger Rastrelli already enjoyed a well-deserved reputation of his own, having gained much experience constructing regal edifices; since 1730 he had served as court architect to Empress Anna Ioannovna (r. 1730–40) and directed work on several palaces and suburban residences, including the third Winter

Palace in St. Petersburg (1732–36). During Empress Elizabeth's reign, Rastrelli was charged with the reconstruction of the imperial country residences at Peterhof and Tsarskoye Selo (1745–57) and erected palaces for leading members of the Russian aristocracy. It was not by chance, then, that this architect, who had already earned the monarch's favor and general acclaim, was entrusted with the difficult task of creating a new imperial palace on the site of the winter residences of the Russian monarchs. In April 1754 the empress signed the Decree on the Construction of the Winter Palace. The new building was to be erected on the site of Empress Anna Ioannovna's Winter Palace, a repeatedly reconstructed ramshackle complex that did not accord with Elizabeth's demanding tastes. The building, which was striking for its sheer size as well as its magnificent architectural decor, was designed in the exceptionally opulent and grand style known as Elizabethan baroque.

The main edifice was complete by 1759, but work continued on the facades and interiors, ending three years later, around the time of the empress's death. Once the palace was completed, the St. Petersburg chief of police, Nikolai Korff, suggested that the new ruler, Peter III, allow the capital's inhabitants to remove all the construction debris that had accumulated in front of the structure. That clever decision cleared the square in a matter of hours—a task that had seemed impossible—and greatly amused the emperor, who watched from a window. After only a brief sojourn in his new residence, Peter was deposed in a coup in June 1762, and his wife, Catherine, acceded to the throne. A German by birth, the former Princess Sophie Friederike Auguste of Anhalt-Zerbst was now empress of Russia.

The rise to power of Catherine II marked a new era in Russian history. Seeking to glorify her reign as an enlightened monarch and following the practices and philosophy of Peter the Great, the empress embarked on a series of reforms and patronage of the arts, enterprises that would earn her the same honorific title as her celebrated predecessor. Within her apartments in the Winter Palace she created a private museum, which she christened her "hermitage," a French word meaning "hermit's dwelling" or "place of solitude." Although today the term is generally used to denote the entire group of the Winter Palace and adjoining buildings, in eighteenth-century court culture, *hermitage* described an isolated park pavilion intended as a place where crowned heads of state and others of high rank could spend time in private. For the sake of privacy, even servants were sometimes forbidden from entering the inner rooms, and ingenious systems were installed to make do without their presence: food and drink were served on ready-laid tables raised through a hatch in the floor by means of a mechanical hoist.

In keeping with established tradition, Catherine's Hermitage in the Winter Palace was devised primarily as a place for the empress to retreat from the affairs and concerns of state. In the 1760s it consisted of four or five rooms, which she referred to as the "Imperial Museum" in letters to her Parisian friend and agent, Baron Melchior Grimm. In 1777, she wrote: "This winter I lodged delightfully well: I have a whole maze of apartments, although I am alone. . . . People have given it the name 'Imperial Museum' and as soon as you go in there you see so much that it's impossible to come out. . . . This Museum is in the corner of the building: it is reached by way of China, China by way of Turkey, that by way of Persia . . . " Like her predecessors, Catherine embarked on a building program of her own. On her orders the Small Hermitage was built in 1764–66 by Yury Veldten to the design of Jean-Baptiste Vallin de la Mothe, who had been given the post of court architect after Rastrelli's departure. It consisted of a hanging garden, two galleries, and two pavilions; the northern pavilion, overlooking the Neva, became the new home of the empress's "Museum." Between 1771 and 1787 she ordered the construction of a larger building next to the Small Hermitage to house the growing art collections and libraries she was acquiring. Originally called the Large Hermitage, the building, which extends as far as the Winter Canal, later became known as the Old Hermitage.

Within this vast architectural ensemble and its ever-expanding collections, Catherine hosted famous parties—both grand and intimate—that became known by the name of their venue. The historian Alexander Uspensky reported that the "large hermitages" held on Thursdays drew more than two hundred eminent guests. "The same persons only in lesser number" were invited to "medium-sized hermitages," and the "small hermitages" were select gatherings of "rarely more than a dozen people," permanent members of the empress's circle and her closest confidants. These included the marshal of the court Prince Fiodor Bariatinsky; Prince Alexander Golitsyn; the lady-in-waiting Anna Protasova; Princess Yekaterina Dashkova; the Austrian field marshal Charles Joseph, Prince de Ligne; and the French and Austrian envoys Louis-Philippe, Comte de Ségur, and Count Ludwig von Cobenzl. "An honor accorded to the few" was how Princess Dashkova described one such invitation. Another contemporary, Count Alexander Ribaupierre, stated that "it was a privilege enjoyed by the courtiers closest to her, but occasionally the empress admitted outsiders to the Hermitage gatherings by way of a rare exception."

In the company of her intimates, Catherine was a charming and cordial hostess. The rules she established called on her guests to, among other things, "leave all ranks outside the doors, like your hats, leave seniority and haughtiness at the door as well, be jolly . . . eat sweet and tasty things, but drink in moderation so that each might find his feet to go out of the door, . . . not wash dirty linen in public, and also not stand before the Empress but treat her as an equal." The program of events often included a visit to the court theater, or Opera House, originally located in the southwest corner of the Winter Palace. The first performance there took place in December 1763, a little over a year after Catherine had assumed the throne, and for two decades the Opera House remained the center of theatrical life in the capital. Then, in 1783, the empress ordered Italian architect Giacomo Quarenghi (1744–1817) to construct a separate theater building on the site of Peter the Great's

Winter Palace, a location that was not chosen at random: As far back as Anna Ioannovna's reign, the old palace, sited at the juncture of the Winter Canal and the Neva embankment, had been used as accommodations for musicians and actors, thus becoming known as the Theatrical House.

The new Hermitage Theater was completed by October 1785, and the first rehearsal was held in the empress's presence as early as November 16. Yet despite the theater's opening on November 22 with a performance of the comic opera *The Miller–Sorcerer, Matchmaker, and Cheat*, work on the facades and interior decoration continued until October 1789. Also during this time, Yury Veldten designed an elevated walkway to connect the theater to the Large Hermitage. In Catherine's time, the Hermitage Theater staged nearly the entire European repertoire of the period—plays by Molière, Beaumarchais, Sheridan, and others—as well as pieces for which the empress wrote the libretto, including comic operas and "historical pageants" such as *The Life of Rurik* and *Oleg's Early Reign*. While the theater was under construction, Catherine wrote ten works for the stage, in collaboration with her secretary of state Alexander Khrapovitsky. Particularly popular was her comic opera *Fevei*, with music by Vasily Pashkevich, which was staged eleven times.

The magnificent theater, where stars of the European and Russian stage shone brightly, became an inseparable dimension of the multifaceted life of the Russian imperial court. The empress invited famous European composers, musicians, actors, and stage designers to her court. Music for her own plays was written by Canobbio, Cimarosa, and Giuseppe Sarti, who succeeded Giovanni Paisiello as court conductor. Beginning in 1792 the design of theatrical productions was entrusted to the outstanding scenographer Pietro Gonzaga, who "amazed the whole city with his exceptional art and at first the sets that he had painted caused the audience to forget about the performance being given, making everyone admire his brush and his intellect, because he is as strong in optics and coloring as he is great in composition."

By this time the Hermitage had begun to transform into a true museum, encompassing a world-class collection of works of art. Indeed, collecting was a matter of international prestige for the empress. By the 1760s the foremost European art collections already had a history dating back two centuries. Catherine looked to examples of crowned collectors among her contemporaries as well, notably King Frederick II of Prussia and Elector Augustus III of Saxony. She was lavish in her acquisitions, expending large amounts primarily out of political considerations and the need to remain true to her reputation as an enlightened monarch.

LEFT

Louis Tocqué. Portrait of Empress Elizabeth. 1758. Oil on canvas. 103 ⅛ x 80 ⅜ in. (262 x 204 cm). One of the most distinguished European portraitists of his day, Tocqué was invited to St. Petersburg specially to paint a gala portrait of the empress. After a few sittings in the palace, the artist produced a grand yet living image of Elizabeth, who is shown with the attributes of monarchy: the orb and sceptre, as well as the badge and sash of the Order of St. Andrew the First-Called.

The Main (Jordan) Staircase in the Winter Palace. Architect: Francesco Bartolomeo Rastrelli, 1754–62; restored 1837–39 (after the fire) under the direction of Vasily Stasov.

The date of the founding of the Hermitage museum is traditionally given as 1764, the year that a collection of 225 western European paintings from Berlin arrived in St. Petersburg. Assembled by the Prussian merchant Johann Ernst Gotzkowsky and originally intended for Frederick the Great, the collection was acquired through the agency of the Russian ambassador Vladimir Dolgoruky.

Earlier in the century Frederick had acquired many superb examples of contemporary French painting, which he installed in the gallery of the Sans-Souci palace in Potsdam. In the mid-1750s he became increasingly interested in Old Masters and asked Gotzkowsky to seek out and purchase valuable works by Italian and Flemish painters. However, as a result of his defeat at the hands of Russian forces during the Seven Years' War, the king was unable to pay for the collection. Gotzkowsky soon found himself on the brink of bankruptcy (among other things, he had issued promissory notes to cover the indemnity imposed on Berlin during its occupation by Russian troops) and suggested to Dolgoruky that he would use the paintings to repay his debt. Although the collection included some second-rate pieces—Gotzkowsky was not an expert on paintings—it also contained many works of exceedingly high quality. Among them were *Portrait of a Young Man Holding a Glove* by Frans Hals, *Family Portrait* by Jacob Jordaens, *New Market in Amsterdam* by Bartholomeus van der Helst, and Jan Steen's *Revelers*. For Catherine II this acquisition represented more than just an important step in the formation of her own imperial collection: She had managed to get the better of "Old Fritz" himself, whose ruinous defeat forced him to forego the purchase of artworks that had been collected at his request. A similar combination of collecting passion and political calculation would feature several more times in the Russian empress's extraordinary biography.

ABOVE, LEFT
Facade of the Small Hermitage. Architect: Jean-Baptiste Vallin de la Mothe, 1764–75.

ABOVE, RIGHT
Facade of the Old Hermitage. Architect: Yury Veldten, 1771–87.

OPPOSITE
*Vigilius Erichsen. Portrait of Catherine II before a Mirror. 1762. Oil on canvas. 105 ¼ x 80 in. (265 x 203 cm).
This Danish artist, who worked at the Russian court between 1757 and 1772, produced some 30 portraits of Catherine II
with different programs, compositions, and purposes. He was the first in Russia to use this type of portrait with a mirror,
making it possible to show the two sides of the subject's character—the imperious monarch and the sensitive woman.*

In the ensuing years, Catherine purposefully created her own picture gallery, following the recommendations of acknowledged experts on art, notably Denis Diderot, François Tronchin, Melchior Grimm, and Johann Friedrich Reifenstein, among many others. The acquisitions of European family collections, which had been astutely assembled by several generations, enhanced Russia's international prestige no less than the Empire's victories on the battlefield.

Beginning in 1765, one of Catherine's most active agents was Prince Dmitry Golitsyn, the Russian ambassador in Paris (and later The Hague). It was Golitsyn who concluded a contract with Étienne Maurice Falconet, the future creator of the bronze equestrian statue of Peter the Great. He also commissioned the still-life with attributes of the arts from Jean-Baptiste Chardin for the St. Petersburg Academy of Arts (now in the Hermitage); negotiated with Carle van Loo and Jean-Baptiste Greuze (whose *Paralytic* was bought for the Hermitage); and maintained close contacts with Diderot. At an auction in Paris, Golitsyn acquired several paintings from Jean de Julienne's collection, most notably *The Doctor's Visit* by Gabriel Metsu. In 1768, before his move to The Hague, the prince purchased from the collection of the Archbishop of Cologne the best of the Hermitage's Rembrandts, *The Return of the Prodigal Son*. Spring that same year saw the acquisition in Brussels of the small but extremely fine collections of Dutch and Flemish works assembled by Prince de Ligne and Count Johann Carl Cobenzl; outstanding among the latter's were *Statue of Ceres* and *Roman Charity* by Peter Paul Rubens. Cobenzl's collection of drawings, purchased at the same time, comprised more than 6,000 works, embracing almost all the European schools. It became the source of most of the sixteenth-century French pencil portraits now in the Hermitage.

Catherine II Receiving a Turkish Embassy on October 14, 1764, in the Audience Chamber of the Neva Enfilade
in the Winter Palace. *Engraving by Andrei Kazachinsky (1794), after a drawing by Mikhail Makhayev and Jean-Louis
De Veilly (1764).*
*When she came to the throne, Catherine II commissioned the architect Jean-Baptiste Vallin de la Mothe to reconstruct the
imperial apartments in the palace built for her predecessor, Elizabeth. The largest of these was the Audience Chamber,
intended for particularly grand receptions and therefore decorated with especial splendor.*

The following year Catherine acquired the Dresden collection of Count Heinrich von Brühl,
the minister of Elector Augustus III of Saxony, who had emulated his sovereign's collecting activities.
After consultations with the eminent art specialist Karl Heinrich von Heikenen and with unlimited
access to the royal treasury, Brühl managed to assemble an outstanding collection. Unfortunately he
also amassed enormous debts, and after his death in 1763 the count's property was sequestered. Five
years later the sequestration was lifted, and Andrei Beloselsky, the Russian envoy to Dresden,
managed to bargain the gallery from Brühl's heirs for 180,000 Dutch guilders. "Everyone here is
amazed at how little it cost us," Beloselsky reported in a letter. In addition to the more than 600
paintings by Dutch, Flemish, French, Italian, and German artists, Brühl's estate contained some
1,500 prints and drawings. The new acquisitions were transported to St. Petersburg via Hamburg on a
specially chartered ship, but on arrival it was discovered that the journey had taken an unfortunate
toll on their condition. Between January and July 1769 Lucas Conrad Pfandzelt, the Hermitage's first
professional restorer, labored to return the works to their original splendor.

The Brühl collection brought into the Hermitage such Dutch and Flemish gems as
Rembrandt's *Portrait of an Old Man in Red*, Rubens's *Perseus and Andromeda*, *Reading a Letter* by
Gerard Terborch, five landscapes by Jacob van Ruisdael, and other masterpieces. Among the Italian
works, besides the views of Dresden and Pirna by Bernardo Bellotto (the artist's own interpretation of
a series first painted for Augustus III), mention should be made of Giovanni Battista Tiepolo's
Maecenas Presenting the Liberal Arts to Emperor Augustus. Painted in the mid-1740s for a

The interior hall of the Hermitage Theater. Architect: Giacomo Quarenghi, 1783–87.
Designed by Giacomo Quarenghi, an Italian architect invited to work in St. Petersburg in 1780, the Hermitage Theater fully reflects Catherine II's fascination with the culture of antiquity. The auditorium takes the form of a Greek amphitheatre with six tiers of benches. The columns placed along the walls feature capitals decorated with theatrical masks, and between them are relief portraits of outstanding ancient dramatists.

commission by Count Francesco Algarotti and presented by him to Brühl as a token of his admiration for the Saxon minister's collecting activities, the work's allegorical message was made transparent by the depiction of Brühl's Dresden palace in the background.

Catherine's acquisitions continued at a rapid rate, often accompanied by complex and delicate negotiations. In 1770 François Tronchin, a legal advisor to the council of Geneva and friend of Voltaire, Diderot, and Grimm, agreed to sell for the enlargement of the Hermitage gallery the collection of paintings that he had acquired in the 1740s and 1750s. The deal was brokered by Diderot and Golitsyn and executed in the name of Ivan Betskoi (1704–1795), one of Catherine's closest associates. This purchase included paintings by David Teniers the Younger, Philips Wouwerman, and Rembrandt. A year later Golitsyn acquired the best paintings from the cabinet of the late Gerrit Braamcamp in Amsterdam, which was styled "the Temple of Art." The 1766 catalogue of this collection mentions works by Terborch, Ostade, Steen, Gerrit Dou, Potter, Adriaen van de Velde, Metsu, and Rembrandt. Unfortunately, the ship on which the purchases were dispatched to the Russian capital sank in the Baltic. Concerned at the impression this tragedy might make in Europe, Catherine coolly wrote in a letter to Voltaire: "A mere 60,000 gold pieces are lost. We shall have to manage without them. This year I have had a few setbacks in similar circumstances. What can one do? Only console oneself."

Consolation was not long in coming. In 1772, on Tronchin's initiative and supported by Diderot and Golitsyn, Catherine purchased the famous picture gallery in Paris that had belonged to Louis-Antoine Crozat, Baron de Thiers, until his death two years earlier. The works formed part of the larger collection assembled by Pierre Crozat (1665–1740), a banker with a superb understanding of painting and close connections in the art world. Pierre bequeathed the collection to his nephew Louis-François Crozat, Marquis du Châtel, after whose death in 1750 most of the works fell into the hands of his brother Louis-Antoine. Negotiations with the baron's heirs, in which Diderot and Tronchin participated, ended with one of the most valuable acquisitions in the history of the Hermitage. The museum gained such masterpieces of the Italian Renaissance as Raphael's *Holy Family*, Titian's *Danae*, Giorgione's *Judith*, and Veronese's *Lamentation* as well as outstanding works by Dutch and Flemish masters, including Rembrandt's *Danae* and *Holy Family*, Rubens's *Bacchus* and *Portrait of a Lady-in-Waiting to the Infanta Isabella*, and six van Dyck portraits. Also acquired were a considerable number of works by French seventeenth- and eighteenth-century artists, including Le Nain, Poussin, Mignard, Watteau, Lancret, and Chardin. The collection, which cost the Russian treasury 460,000 livres, was delivered to St. Petersburg by sea in June 1772.

At nearly the same moment Catherine staged yet one more coup. While the empress's agents were negotiating the purchase of the Crozat gallery, the collection of Etienne-François, Duc de Choiseul, came up for auction. Sent into retirement and confined to his estate of Chanteloup, the disgraced statesman was obliged to part with his collection (which included another share of the Crozat gallery inherited by the Duchesse de Choiseul, née Louise-Honorine Crozat du Châtel). Acting on the empress's behalf at the auction, Diderot managed to secure for the Hermitage eleven

Peter Paul Rubens. Perseus and Andromeda. *Ca. 1632. Oil on canvas. 39 ⅛ x 54 ¾ in. (99.5 x 139 cm).*
This painting came into the Hermitage in 1769, part of Heinrich's Brühl's collection from Dresden, making it one of the
museum's first, as well as one of its best, works by Rubens. Certain elements in the presentation of the mythological subject
may seem superfluous: in order to arrive in time to rescue the princess being sacrificed to the terrible monster, either the
winged sandals alone or the magical horse Pegasus would have been enough. Still, together the details form a rich yet
exceptionally balanced composition extolling the triumph of love.

paintings, including *Deer Hunt* by Wouwerman and *The Doctor's Visit* by Gerard Dou. For
Catherine this acquisition from Choiseul, who in the twelve years of his ascendancy had pursued
policies hostile to Russia, surely harbored a small act of revenge. The removal of the Crozat and
Choiseul collections to St. Petersburg caused a great stir in Paris, particularly because Catherine
made these expensive acquisitions while Russia was engaged in a long drawn-out war against the
Turks (1768–74). As Diderot wrote to Falconet: "The connoisseurs are howling, the artists are
howling, the wealthy are howling. . . . The empress intends to acquire the Thiers collection during a
ruinous war: that is what humiliates and embarrasses them."

Despite such warnings, acquisitions continued apace, launching Catherine into the ranks of
Europe's preeminent collectors. An event of tremendous import in the history of the Hermitage was
the purchase of 198 paintings from the famed gallery of Sir Robert Walpole, British prime minister
under George I and George II. Dubbed "the missionary of vice" by Lord Bolingbroke for his bribery
of members of parliament, Walpole was among the greatest English collectors of the first half of the
eighteenth century. The gems of his collection were concentrated at the family seat, Houghton Hall

Luca Giordano. Vulcan's Forge. Ca. 1660. Oil on canvas. 75 ¾ x 59 ⅝ in. (192.5 x 151.5 cm).
*This canvas, which entered the Hermitage in 1779 as part of the Walpole collection, is a splendid example of Giordano's
early work. The artist seems to be showing us how beautiful a picture can be simply because its creator has a perfect
command of all the elements of painting: expressive line and composition, lifelike depiction of the human body in the most
complex poses and movements, nuances of lighting.*

P. 25
The Raphael Loggias in the New Hermitage. Architect: Giacomo Quarenghi. 1780s.

in Norfolk. In 1778 the statesman's grandson George Walpole offered the entire Houghton Hall collection to Catherine, through the intermediary Alexei Musin-Pushkin, Russian ambassador in London. Despite opposition in England and even attempts to organize a subscription to buy the collection for the nation, Catherine acquired it for 40,000 pounds; the paintings arrived in St. Petersburg in the autumn of 1779.

In common with other major collections assembled by English aristocrats, Walpole's consisted chiefly of works by seventeenth-century Italian artists as well as paintings by Rubens, van Dyck, and Poussin. His gallery brought into the Hermitage Luca Giordano's *Bacchus* and *Vulcan's Forge*, Guido Reni's *Dispute of the Church Fathers*, and Salvator Rosa's *Prodigal Son*. The collection of Flemish painting was also considerably enriched through the addition of Rubens's *Landscape with Stone-Haulers*, *Feast at the House of Simon the Pharisee*, and designs for triumphal arches, along with the *Madonna with Partridges* and portraits from van Dyck's London period as well as the four *Market Stalls* and *Bird Concert* by Snyders. Among the masterworks from other national schools were *The Holy Family* and *Moses Striking the Rock for Water* by Poussin, *The Immaculate Conception* and *Adoration of the Shepherds* by Murillo, and Rembrandt's *Sacrifice of Isaac*. These were joined by works purchased from another notable English collection, that of Robert Udney, which added Guido Reni's *Rape of Europa* to the Russian imperial picture gallery.

The last major acquisition of the eighteenth century was the collection of 119 mostly Dutch and Flemish paintings owned by Count Baudouin. When Catherine's friend and agent Melchior Grimm initially brought the collection to her attention, he stressed that it was known to all Russians who visited Paris. Negotiations over the sale lasted four years and nearly broke down; finally, in 1783, the entire collection was added to the Hermitage's already impressive stores, which now boasted nine more Rembrandts (including *Portrait of an Old Jew*, *Portrait of an Old Woman*, *Portrait of the Poet Jeremias de Decker*, and *Young Woman Trying on Earrings*) and additional works by van Dyck, Ostade, Jacob van Ruisdael, and David Teniers the Younger.

The story of Catherine the Great's formation of the Hermitage collection contains many fascinating pages, but one of the most striking concerns the Raphael Loggias. In 1778 Catherine wrote to Grimm of her complete enchantment with the Vatican's frescoes, created in 1517–19 by Raphael and his pupils for Pope Leo X, which she had seen reproduced in color prints by Volpato and Ottaviani. She wanted to commission something similar for Russia. At the empress's request, Grimm contacted the amateur archaeologist Johann Friedrich Reifenstein, a close associate of Johann Joachim Winckelmann who was living in Rome, to ask him to organize the copying of the original frescoes. The Russian diplomat Nikolai Yusupov obtained permission from Pope Pius VI, and work in the Vatican Palace was soon under way.

The group of artists that Reifenstein recruited for the empress's commission was led by Austrian painter Christoph Unterberger (1731–1798), a pupil and associate of Anton Raphael Mengs (1728–1779), with whom he had painted the Vatican library. Rather than using the technique of fresco, it was decided to reproduce the original compositions in egg tempera on canvases, which would then be mounted to the walls and ceilings of the gallery prepared for them at the Hermitage. Certain deviations from the originals were dictated by political considerations (for example, the shield bearing the arms of Leo X was replaced by a double-headed eagle with Catherine's monogram), and the stuccowork in the Vatican loggias was imitated in the Hermitage by painting in the grisaille technique. The finished copies were exhibited at the Quirinal Palace in Rome in August 1780, after which they were dispatched in sections to Livorno, where Russian naval ships stood ready to transport them to St. Petersburg.

Meanwhile, of the ensuing expansion along the Winter Canal to accommodate the works, Catherine wrote: "For want of other suggestions, we have the intention of joining the buildings of the Hermitage with loggias placed along the canal . . . towards Shepelev's house." The loggias were created by Giacomo Quarenghi, whose arrival in Russia was also the work of Reifenstein; in 1792 the Vatican copies took their place in the new building. The reproductions were remarkably faithful to the originals, as noted in 1839 by Eugen Hess, the son of the Bavarian battle-painter Peter Hess who visited St. Petersburg with his father at Nicolas I's invitation. He remarked that "very attractive too is the copy of Raphael's Vatican loggias that were made by some Russian almost like the real thing."

Quarenghi's loggias were left nearly untouched until the mid-nineteenth century, when Emperor Nicholas I embarked on the creation of the New Hermitage, Russia's first public art museum. At that time, they were reconstructed and incorporated into the complex being erected according to the design of Leo von Klenze, court architect of King Ludwig I of Bavaria. During the construction of this new repository for the imperial collections, the tempera paintings were removed from the walls, damaged areas were restored, and the gilding was reapplied. Although the architecture that surrounds these unusual works has changed, they still occupy the same gallery in the Hermitage that Catherine II chose for them.

Guided by both personal taste and political aspirations, throughout the last quarter of the eighteenth century the empress carefully shaped her collection in St. Petersburg, nearly doubling the holdings of paintings from 2,080 in 1774 to 3,996 in 1797. Yet the picture gallery was only part of the imperial collection. In a letter to Grimm dated September 18, 1790, the empress reported with satisfaction that "My museum in the Hermitage consists, not counting the paintings and Raphael loggias, of 38,000 books, four rooms filled with books and prints, 10,000 cameos and intaglios, roughly 10,000 drawings and a natural science collection that fills two large halls." Such voracious acquiring was sometimes regarded as indiscriminate and judged with disfavor by contemporaries; the Prince de Ligne, who knew the empress well, stated that "she had no understanding of painting." Indeed, it was no secret that Catherine's true passion was cameos, on which she was prepared to spend huge sums. One such expenditure came in the summer of 1779, when she bought from Mengs's collection the *Perseus and Andromeda* cameo, a treasure that had proved too expensive even for King Charles III of Spain. Another significant acquisition was the nearly 1,500 carved stones purchased in 1787 from the family collection of the Ducs d'Orléans, a junior branch of the French royal family. Described by a contemporary as "one of the prime memorabilia of the Hermitage," the purchase cost the imperial treasury some 40,000 rubles. In 1792 the glyptic collection of Giovanni Battista Casanova, the brother of the famous adventurer, was bought in Dresden, and the collection of Joseph Angelo de France, custodian of the Antikenkabinett in Vienna, brought another 2,337 items into the Russian empress's possession.

Catherine lavished exceptional care on this part of her private museum. She ordered that everything be catalogued, an undertaking completed for the gems and cameos by 1795 by Alexander Luzhkov. She also commissioned German furniture maker David Roentgen to craft special cabinets decorated with gilded bronze for the storage of cameos and medals. The artist and chemist Georg König and the engraver Karl Lebrecht worked in the empress's apartments to create glass copies of the pieces. (Many reproductions of European glyptic collections were ordered from abroad.) Her desire for gems became well known throughout the West, and Catherine herself only half-jokingly referred to her obsession with cameo collecting as a "disease." Of her collection of 10,000 carved stones and 40,000 glass copies, she wrote on April 6, 1795: "All the collections in Europe are mere children's playthings compared to Ours."

In contrast to the abundance of paintings, graphic arts, and glyphic collections, Catherine's Hermitage contained hardly any sculpture. The greater part of acquisitions in this field was kept at her suburban residence of Tsarskoye Selo. Particularly noteworthy are the items from the collection of John Lyde Browne, bought in 1787, which laid the foundation for the Hermitage's stocks of ancient sculpture. Over the course of forty years this English banker, nicknamed "il Virtuoso" for his appreciation of artistic excellence, bought sculptures from antiquarians, archaeologists, and palazzi owners in Italy. The entirety of his collection, encompassing more than three hundred works, was delivered to Tsarskoye Selo, where it adorned the Grotto pavilion in the park and Catherine's apartments in the Great Palace. Certain reliefs and marble tombstones were placed in the Pyramid, next to which the empress buried her favorite dogs.

Although most of Catherine's acquisitions—whether of entire collections, individual works, or her own commissions—were conducted according to established protocol, the empress's advisors sometimes encouraged her to boldly disregard accepted standards of behavior. Such was the case in

Luigi Premazzi. The Room of Coins and Medals in the New Hermitage. *1853. Watercolor and ceruse on paper.*
12 ¾ x 15 ⅞ in. (32.3 x 40.2 cm).
The foundation for the collection of coins and medals that now forms the numerically largest section of the museum's stocks
was laid by Catherine II's numerous acquisitions. Leo von Klenze allotted it a hall on the lower floor of the New Hermitage
that is no less grand than the museum's halls dedicated to antiquities, painting, and sculpture.

the acquisition of the painting *Perseus and Andromeda* by Mengs, which had been exhibited in Rome to great public acclaim. Mengs, one of the founders of neoclassicism whom Winckelmann had pronounced "the greatest artist of his own and the coming age," was enjoying tremendous popularity at the time, and this new work was commissioned and paid for by a private individual in London, a wealthy Welshman named Sir Watkin Williams-Wynn. After the exhibition, the painting was loaded aboard a ship bound for Britain but was captured by pirates off the French coast. The French authorities confiscated the masterpiece, and at Grimm's suggestion it was offered to the Russian empress. On May 18, 1779, Catherine wrote to Grimm: "I see that in order to give me pleasure you intend to rob an honest English gentleman. . . . My conscience troubles me a little that this will be done to the detriment of my neighbor. If the good gentleman contacts me I shall give the painting over to him." He never did.

The empress herself fell victim to unscrupulous dealers. British artist Thomas Jenkins, who with Gavin Hamilton was one of the greatest experts on the antiquities market in Rome, sold Catherine a set of paintings supposedly by Correggio. When it emerged that they were not genuine, an infuriated empress forbade her agents Grimm and Reifenstein to deal with Jenkins (although her son, Paul, worked with the artist on his own acquisitions). With this incident fresh in her mind, the empress later declined the opportunity to acquire a colossal statue of Jupiter discovered during excavations of Emperor Domitian's villa at Castel Gandolfo.

Despite setbacks such as these, Catherine's Hermitage continued to expand exponentially, rapidly outgrowing the isolated pavilion for private dinner parties and the personal study of the enlightened connoisseur. It developed gradually into a tremendous museum of classical art. Catherine's contemporaries soon noted that the museum's grand scale was at odds with its modest name: "The sight of this Hermitage accorded not at all with its title, because on entering one's eyes were struck by the immensity of its halls and galleries, the richness of the furnishings, and the many paintings by great masters." Their unique presentation was also remarked upon. In his 1794 *Description of the Capital City of St. Petersburg*, Johann Gottlieb Georgi wrote: "The paintings . . . are placed not so much in the exact order of schools, artists and so on, as according to visual effect and fit, by which means not only are many paintings accommodated in a small space but also a highly pleasant sight is produced that is changed sometimes by the rearrangement of the paintings." Nevertheless, during Catherine's reign attempts were already under way to systematize the collections, and between 1773 and 1783 the first two-volume handwritten catalogue of the Hermitage gallery was compiled by Count Johann Ernst Münnich.

Despite Catherine the Great's ambitious program to create a showcase for the whole of Europe as well as the Russian people, for many decades her collection remained closed to all but the highest echelons of society. Nevertheless, the legacy of this extraordinary ruler left a lasting impression. As recorded by Astolphe, Marquis de Custine, who visited St. Petersburg forty years after Catherine the Great's death and was received at the court of her grandson Nicholas I: "An inexplicable sorrow reigns in the palace turned into a museum after the death of the person who gave it life by her presence and knew how to live in it to good purpose. That lady autocrat knew better than any the value of a private life and of unforced conversation." It fell to her heirs to carry on.

Catherine the Great's successors did indeed continue the work of expanding the imperial collections, each according to personal tastes and changing political landscapes. Her son, Paul I (r. 1796–1801), abandoned the Winter Palace—a residence inextricably bound up with the memory of a mother who had deposed his father, Peter III, and for many years kept him, the rightful heir to the throne, at a distance. The new emperor surrounded himself with works of art at his favorite residences of Pavlovsk and Gatchina, in the palace on Kamenny (Stone) Island, and for his new residence in St. Petersburg, St Michael's Castle. While still heir to the throne, Paul had bought, through Thomas Jenkins and Bartolomeo Cavaceppi, genuine antiquities unearthed in Italy, including a marble head of Hera (now in the Hermitage) found at Pontanello in 1769 by the archaeologist Gavin Hamilton. As emperor, Paul commissioned from the Carrara workshop of Paolo Andrea Triscorni (1757–1833) a considerable number of marble copies of ancient sculptural masterpieces; he had seen many of the originals, including the *Laocoön* (Vatican collection) and *The Dying Gladiator* (Capitoline Museum in Rome), during his European journey in 1781–82. Triscorni was also engaged to produce original sculptural compositions to adorn the interior of St. Michael's Castle. In June 1797 the paired groups *Diana and Endymion* and *Cupid and Psyche* were delivered from Italy; in the mid-1800s they were moved to the vestibule of the Winter Palace, where they remain. Among the most significant paintings acquired by Paul are *The Union of Earth and Water* by Rubens and *The Farmer's Children* by Fragonard.

After the assassination of Paul during a palace coup on the night of March 11, 1801, the crown passed to his eldest son, Catherine's beloved grandson Alexander I (r. 1801–25). The young autocrat reinstated the Winter Palace as the chief imperial residence and continued his grandmother's course: He bestowed on the Hermitage the status of palace museum and opened its doors to the public. (It should be noted that certain groups, notably pupils of the Academy of Arts, had been granted access to the palace's picture gallery even during Catherine's reign, making the Hermitage ahead of its time compared to more restrictive museums in Europe.) Alexander I, following the liberal tendencies of an era marked by increased interest in artistic life among society in general, declared in 1801: "I desired . . . to show my particular attention to the fine arts and to encourage their spread in Russia."

Alexander's tastes, shaped under the influence of the French Enlightenment and the ideals of Sentimentalism and Classicism, inspired his first acquisitions. In 1802 the emperor bought two paintings by Hubert Robert that had been exhibited at the Paris Salon of 1798: *Arch of a Bridge over a Stream* and *An Ancient Building Used as a Public Bathhouse*. Later, with the aid of Count Alexander Stroganov, he acquired eight more paintings from the French artist, adding to the purchase price a valuable diamond and a diploma of honorary membership in the St. Petersburg Academy of Arts. In this same period the Hermitage was enriched by five paintings by another fashionable artist, the seascape painter Claude-Joseph Vernet. Alexander was cautious, however, in giving opinions on art. According to his adjutant, Alexander Mikhailovsky-Danilevsky, "the Emperor is not a lover of the fine arts and sometimes himself says that he is no expert on them."

Despite his lack of expertise, Alexander continued a policy of acquisitions for the Hermitage gallery. In 1808 Franz Labensky, the curator of the picture gallery (from 1805 officially known as the Second Section of the Imperial Hermitage), was dispatched on an official mission to Paris, where he acquired Caravaggio's *Lute-Player*, Pieter de Hooch's *Woman and a Maid*, and *The Martyrdom of the Apostle Peter* (attributed to Lionello Spada). It was also during this time that the emperor enlisted the aid of the famous Dominique Vivant, Baron Denon, Napoleon's director general of museums, to enlarge the Hermitage collection. Among the paintings Denon bought for St. Petersburg were *Jacob's Dream* by Murillo, *The Appearance of the Virgin to St Lawrence* by Guercino, and a *Deposition* by Luca Giordano.

The most significant expansion of the Hermitage's stocks under Alexander I came with the victorious end of the Napoleonic Wars and the triumphant entry of Russian troops into Paris in 1814. The Russian tsar greatly impressed the Parisians with his courteousness and humanity, managing to protect the French capital from excessive reparations demanded by the commander of the allied Prussian army, Marshal Blücher. Alexander further sought to ease the terms of the peace treaty, demonstrating great sympathy for the vanquished, including members of Napoleon's family. He visited former empress Josephine several times at her home Malmaison, just outside Paris. The suburban chateau, purchased soon after her marriage to Napoleon, was Josephine's favorite residence, and it was there that she had assembled a remarkable collection of paintings and sculpture, some of which were war trophies that Napoleon had presented to his wife. Alexander later ensured that Malmaison would pass to her heirs. As a token of her gratitude, Josephine presented to the Russian emperor the famous Gonzaga cameo that depicts King Ptolemy II Philadelphus of Egypt and his consort Arsinoë II.

During the Treaty of Paris negotiations, Alexander insisted that works of art that had entered French museums as Napoleonic trophies should remain in the country. Yet when Russian forces entered Paris a second time, in 1815, Alexander accepted the offer of Hortense de Beauharnais, daughter of the former French empress, to sell him the Malmaison painting collection. A curious historical twist is connected with this purchase: In 1806 some three hundred paintings from the Kassel gallery were requisitioned for the Musée Napoléon in the Louvre. Despite the orders of Elector William I of Hesse-Kassel to hide forty-eight of the most valuable works, Napoleon's general Lagrange found the paintings and sent them to Empress Josephine. It was a portion of these works that Alexander I acquired from Malmaison. In response to the elector's indignant protests, the tsar agreed to return the canvases if their former owner compensated him the nearly one million francs paid for them. As expected, William declared that he had no intention of paying twice for his own paintings.

Among the masterpieces acquired from Malmaison are Andrea del Sarto's *Holy Family*, *Depositions* by Rembrandt and by Rubens, a series of works by Claude Lorrain devoted to the hours of the day, Terborch's *Glass of Lemonade*, Metsu's *Breakfast*, and Potter's *Farm*. The popularity of this last work in this period is attested in a diary entry made by Eugen Hess, who visited the Hermitage in 1839: "The world-famous p[eeing] cow by Paul Potter is an exceptional picture." Also of great significance for the museum was the addition of four statues by the celebrated neoclassical sculptor Antonio Canova: *Hebe*, *Paris*, *A Dancer*, and *Cupid and Psyche*.

At almost the same time, the Hermitage came into possession of the collection of British banker William Coesvelt, which Alexander I purchased in Amsterdam for 100,000 guilders. This acquisition significantly enhanced the stocks of Spanish painting, which until then was quite poorly represented.

The Hermitage gallery was now enriched by such outstanding works as Velázquez's *Portrait of Olivares*, Zurbarán's *Girlhood of the Virgin*, Puga's *Knife-Grinder*, and a still-life by Pereda.

Despite its status as a palace museum during Alexander I's reign, the Hermitage was not yet a public museum in the true sense. In 1804 Count Dmitry Buturlin had drawn up a program for the reorganization of the Hermitage collection that stressed the social significance of the museum and expressed thoughts about opening it to the public; nonetheless, he insisted on the necessity of preserving its status as a palace institution. Even in 1827, by which time Nicholas I (another grandson of Catherine II; r. 1825–55) had assumed the throne, the Russian response to a request for information from Berlin stressed that "the Hermitage is not a public museum, but an extension of the imperial palace." The Marquis de Custine probably had a similar thought when he wrote of the Hermitage picture gallery: "This gallery is splendid, but it seems to me it is lost in a city where too few people can enjoy it."

Before the Hermitage could truly open its doors to the public, disaster struck: The Winter Palace was gutted by fire. The blaze broke out on the evening of December 17, 1837, caused by a malfunctioning stove flue. The situation was worsened by the use of wood as the primary building material throughout the palace. One eyewitness to the tragedy, court chamberlain Alexander Bashutsky, left a vivid description of the conflagration that raged for more than a day. "The last hours of the phoenix building were grandly mournful. . . . We watched through the broken windows as the fire strolled victorious in the empty space, illuminating the broad passageways: at one moment it cracked and tossed down the marble columns, at another it impudently blackened the precious gilding, the next it fused the crystal and bronze decorative chandeliers together in deformed heaps and then tore the sumptuous brocades and damasks from the walls." The emperor personally directed the staff and guards rescuing the palace's artistic treasures; they barely managed to evacuate the portraits from the gallery of the heroes of the 1812 war against Napoleon. Catherine II's Old Hermitage was saved only by rapidly erecting a protective wall and dousing it with water. The unprecedented blaze destroyed the magnificent decor of the imperial residence, completely consuming the upper two floors.

Faced with the overwhelming devastation, the emperor was determined to rebuild. The palace was reconstructed in record time, with work completed by 1839. Reports appeared condemning the extraordinary pace of rebuilding, including one penned by the Marquis de Custine, who wrote that "the emperor has raised one of the world's greatest palace from the ruins in a single year and [Russians] believe that the death of a few thousand workers, sacrificed to autocratic impatience, to the whim of the emperor posing as the need of the nation, is a mere trifle and not at all an expensive price for this infantile delight." Although this assessment is inaccurate (the tradition of inflating such statistics dates back to descriptions of the construction of St. Petersburg made by European observers in the early 1700s), the working conditions were indeed extremely harsh and the loss of life among the peasant workers regrettable.

The Winter Palace fire interrupted the reconstruction of the imperial museum already under way. The need to expand the museum's premises to accommodate the growth of the collection had long been evident, and in the 1820s and 1830s the question of constructing a new gallery was repeatedly raised. Architects Ludwig Charlemagne, Smaragd Shustov, and Alexander Briullov had offered their visions for the structure, and Vasily Stasov, who directed the reconstruction after the fire, was later asked to examine the previous designs and draw up his own. Yet none of the proposals accorded with the scale of the museum envisioned by Nicholas I.

While traveling through Germany in 1838, Nicholas had visited the new museum buildings constructed in Munich for King Ludwig I of Bavaria to house his rich collections of ancient and modern sculpture and fine paintings: the Glyptothek (opened in 1830) and (Alte) Pinakothek (1836). Nicholas was accompanied on these visits by the creator of these public edifices, Leo von Klenze. So impressed was the Russian emperor by Klenze's basic idea—to produce an architectural and decorative ensemble that formed a fitting setting for the collections contained within—that he invited the architect to Russia and commissioned him to design a museum building in St. Petersburg.

The New Hermitage would house the imperial collections of painting and sculpture, ancient artifacts, drawings and prints, and coins, medals, and cameos.

As early as July 1839 Klenze's "Proposal for the structure of the museum" was approved, citing a completion date of 1846. The architectural plans were examined by a specially formed commission led by the Minister of the Court, Prince Piotr Volkonsky, and the Chief Administrator of Public Institutions, Count Piotr Kleinmichel, and including the leading Russian architects Briullov, Stasov, and Nikolai Yefimov. Construction began in 1840 and continued twelve long years, during which time Klenze repeatedly visited St. Petersburg. His relationship with the Russian architects implementing his design was strained. Stasov, who oversaw construction (succeeded on his death in 1848 by Yefimov), modified Klenze's plan in significant ways, including building materials, the strength of the structure, and questions of economy as well as aspects of layout and planning. To the Bavarian architect, used to an independent privileged position, such modifications were an unwelcome intrusion. The final decision, however, rested with their illustrious client, whose imperial will the architects dared not oppose. On a number of points Klenze was forced to concede to Stasov's proposals, but he categorically rejected changes that, according to him, harmed the "poetry, beauty, and true regularity of the designs."

The site for the New Hermitage was to be in immediate proximity to the Winter Palace, on a plot situated between Millionnaya Street, the Small Hermitage, and the Winter Canal. Klenze initially proposed demolishing everything that stood in the way, including Catherine II's Large Hermitage and the Raphael Loggias block. At the commission's insistence, however, the Large Hermitage was spared (depriving the museum of its northern suite of halls and a facade overlooking

Boris Grin. The Winter Palace Fire of December 17, 1837. 1838. Watercolor on paper. 9 ¾ x 13 ½ in. (24.7 x 34.2 cm).

the Neva), and the Raphael Loggias were incorporated into the new building, becoming an integral part of the New Hermitage.

The formal opening of the museum took place on February 5, 1852. The official festivities were described by Florian Gilles, head of the imperial libraries and the First Section of the Hermitage: "All that splendor and richness in combination with art might present in union shone at that celebration. The brilliance of the event was elevated by the infinite skill with which they decorated and lit the halls where dinner was laid for 600 persons as a conclusion to the festivities. The Spanish hall, containing the table for the imperial family and those of the court ladies and senior officials, presented a wonderful sight. Thousands of candles rising in pyramids above huge lapis-lazuli vases comprised the chief adornment of this hall, and lit with their reflection the magnificent works of Murillo, Velázquez, and other painters. The Italian, van Dyck, and Rubens halls, with their huge vases and candelabra of malachite and jasper—the products of the Urals and Altai—were lit almost as splendidly and allotted to the other guests."

In December of that year the emperor commissioned academician Konstantin Ukhtomsky and artists Eduard Hau and Luigi Premazzi to paint watercolors recording the halls and exteriors of the New Hermitage. These works, executed between 1852 and 1861 and bound together in an album, present the appearance of the Imperial Museum as it was conceived and realized by its creators, serving as visual proof that the interiors of Russia's first art museum have been preserved almost unchanged to the present day. Thanks to the exquisitely rendered, detailed depictions, we know that the most sumptuous areas were the three central halls on the upper floor known as the Skylight Halls, in which were displayed works by Spanish, Flemish, and Italian artists. These were lit from above, an innovation in museum construction at the time; the placement of a glazed lantern in a vaulted ceiling gave the added benefit of allowing the rays of light reflected off the vault to be distributed evenly across the walls. Also noteworthy was the creation of a hall dedicated to Russian painting, in which shone the creations of Karl Briullov, Fiodor Bruni, and Alexander Ivanov. In 1897 these works were moved to the Russian Museum in St. Petersburg (housed in the former palace of Grand Duke Mikhail, Nicholas I's brother), which opened to the public in 1898.

The three flights of the grand marble staircase lead to a "fore-hall" (now the Van Dyck Hall), which Klenze originally proposed to decorate with frescoes on the theme of Russian history; unfortunately, climatic conditions forced the abandonment of this plan. The hall at the top of the grand staircase was called the Gallery of the History of Ancient Painting, and for its decoration the Bavarian artist Georg Hiltensperger, a pupil of Peter Joseph von Cornelius, produced a series of eighty-six paintings on copper sheets, which were set into the walls. These were executed in encaustic (a wax-based painting medium), a technique that originated in classical Antiquity and that the artist had studied in Pompeii and Naples. Many of these paintings re-create lost works by Greek and Roman artists that are known only from written descriptions. Klenze had created a similar series for the Pinakothek in Munich, although there the artist took subjects from the history of Italian and German painting. The practice was not uncommon in Europe, dating back to the Renaissance, whose artists had sought to re-create lost easel paintings from classical Antiquity. In his time the German writer Johann Wolfgang Goethe had tried to inspire Weimar artists to reproduce the images described in the *Eikones* (*Images*) by the Sophist Philostratos. He wrote: "The Herculanean, Pompeian, and other rediscovered pictures, particularly the mosaics, enable us to travel in spirit and imagination to that period of art. This attempt is very pleasing and praiseworthy as the artists of recent times have worked very little in that direction." Like many of his contemporaries, Goethe

LEFT
The Malachite Room in the Winter Palace. Architect: Alexander Briullov, 1837–39. The idea of finishing classical-style interiors with Russian semiprecious stone was first realized by Catherine II in the Agate Rooms at Tsarskoye Selo. In the early 19th century, attractive minerals from the Urals, above all malachite, became famous throughout Europe. Under Nicholas I this hall, superbly reworked by Alexander Briullov (the original project was by Montferrand), became the chief state drawing-room in the apartments of Empress Alexandra Fiodorovna.

believed in the possibility and usefulness of re-creating lost works of ancient easel painting on the basis of ancient descriptions, in conjunction with surviving frescoes and mosaics uncovered by the excavations at Pompeii.

The Hermitage gallery is unparalleled in the scope of its historical reconstruction: Unfolding before the viewer is the full chronicle of ancient painting (as imagined in the mid-nineteenth century, on the basis of written sources). The chief source for the program of works drawn up by Klenze was Pliny the Elder's *Natural History*. Fifty-one of the eighty-six subjects derive from Pliny; five were taken from the Greek writer Athenaeus, and four each from the works of Strabo, Pausanias, and Lucian. Apart from the re-creations of works by ancient painters (*Sleeping Cyclops* by Timanthes, *Medea* by Timomachus, *A Family of Centaurs* by Zeuxis), the pictures in the gallery present anecdotal episodes from the biographies of artists, such as Panaenus, Parrhasius, and Apelles. Later, European sculpture was brought into this hall, along with decorative works made of

The portico of the New Hermitage, with figures of atlantes by the sculptor Alexander Terebenev, 1844–49.

Russian semiprecious stone: tabletops, vases, and mosaics created at Peterhof, in the Urals and Altai mountains.

For the decoration of the facades of the New Hermitage, Klenze devised an original approach, embellishing them with sculptures of twenty-eight major personages in the arts, from ancient times to the early nineteenth century. The models for the sculptures were produced in Munich by the same sculptors who had collaborated with the Bavarian architect during the construction of the Glyptothek and Pinakothek: Ludwig Michael Schwanthaler and Johann Leeb, among others. The models were delivered to St. Petersburg, where Russian sculptors produced full-sized versions, from which the sculptures were cast in a lead-zinc alloy. The subjects are Daedalus (representing architecture); Winckelmann (representing archaeology and art history); Marcantonio Raimondi and Raphael Morghen (engravers); Pyrgoteles, Dioscorides, and Pichler (carvers of gemstones); Onata, Smilis, Phidias, Polyclitus, Scopas, Michelangelo, and Benvenuto Cellini (sculptors); Timanthes, Polygnotus, Zeuxis, Apelles, and Parrhasius (ancient painters); Raphael, Leonardo da Vinci, Rembrandt, Adriaen van Ostade, Correggio, Titian, van Dyck, Rubens, and Dürer (painters from the Renaissance onward). Their placement on the museum's exterior corresponded to the location of the collections inside. On the lower story, facing Millionnaya Street, the statues of the archaeologist and engravers marked the site of the library, with its collections of books, manuscripts, and prints, while the figures of Rubens and van Dyck marked that of the painting displays inside. For the museum's south portico, Russian sculptor Alexander Terebenev produced a tour de force: ten colossal atlantes (called "telamons" or "caryatids" in museum documents) carved from grey Serdobol granite. He

Large Skylight Hall in the New Hermitage. Architect: Leo von Klenze, with the participation of Vasily Stasov and Nicolas Yefimov, 1851.
One of the three largest halls in the New Hermitage, the Hall of the Italian Schools got its other name—the Large Skylight Hall—from the glazed ceiling conceived by Klenze and implemented by the Russian architect Pavel Ochakov. Thanks to the lighting from above and the concentration of the stucco decoration on the ceiling, the room's palatial splendor does not clash with its function of displaying works of art.

began work on the commission in 1844, undertaking to complete the colossal statues in just two years (in fact it took twice as long). With Klenze's consent, he changed the original design, based on a model by Johann Halbig, including adding ears of grain to the heads. The finished works gained the approval of Nicholas I, who awarded Terebenev with the title of academician and a diamond ring; his assistants (120 stonemasons) received five silver rubles each. Klenze remarked that "with regard to true artistic value and beauty, [the New Hermitage atlantes] in many ways surpass . . . everything known of this kind."

Working in the new style known as Neo-Grecian, Klenze managed to create an integrated museum complex in which all the elements—from the lighting to the interior decoration—were carefully thought out and executed in accordance with the exhibits displayed within. Even the cases and stands were produced by Russian craftsmen working from drawings made by the architect. Like

Peter the Great and his Kunstkammer, Nicholas I took great pride in the creation of Russia's first public museum, which he considered an adornment of his reign. When the dark days of the Crimean War (1853–56) caused him to review his achievements, he became fond of walking through the museum's halls, declaring, "Yes, it truly is beautiful!"

The emperor was not merely the creator of the new museum; he also directed the commission responsible for selecting and hanging the works. In his youth, Nicholas had taken painting lessons from Professor Alexander Sauerweid of the Academy of Arts and considered himself thoroughly competent in questions of aesthetics. "By my position in the state, I should be the first artist in the country," the autocratic monarch once declared. In the catalogue of paintings that belonged to Nicholas is this entry: "Flemish school landscape. In the foreground Russian cavalrymen . . . Van Goyen. Landscape. Russian troop manoeuvres. Figures added by His Imperial Majesty the Emperor while still a Grand Duke." It was during his reign that the "tapestry" method of hanging paintings, customary since Catherine the Great's day, was abandoned in favor of a more art-historical approach. The 1851 regulations state that "symmetrical order" is preferable, "but only in as far as this is really possible and without any disruption of a historically correct placement of items." He interfered unabashedly in the work of the architects, decorators, and painters laboring on his commissions, and he displayed no less arbitrary self-assurance concerning the composition of the collection.

Nicholas is often criticized for instructing the sale of paintings from the Hermitage. It is indeed true that at several auctions in 1854 more than 1,200 paintings, deemed to have no great value for the gallery or for the adornment of the palace interiors, were sold. The selection was made by a commission chaired by academician Fiodor Bruni, who from 1849 acted as curator of the Hermitage picture gallery. The auctions brought in a total of 16,500 rubles, or less than 14 rubles for each painting sold. It should be noted, however, that this occurrence was far from unprecedented in museum practice at the time. Two years earlier, some one thousand paintings from the Munich Pinakothek had been sold for 6,000 guilders, and in 1856 three hundred paintings from the Budapest gallery brought the Hungarian crown a profit of 700 florins. Generally items of relatively low value were chosen for sale, but among the paintings auctioned from the Hermitage was more than one significant work, such as Chardin's *Still Life with Attributes of the Arts* (which passed through three private collections in St. Petersburg before returning to the museum in 1924). This sad fact must be attributed to insufficient competence on the part of the commission that, in addition to Bruni, included the distinguished painters Piotr Basin and Timofei Neff (the latter was appointed curator of the Hermitage picture gallery in 1864).

Despite such unfortunate events, the New Hermitage became a treasure-house worthy of the masterpieces whose numbers Nicholas, following the example of his grandmother and elder brother, sought to increase. Indeed, his reign saw a succession of important acquisitions that considerably enriched the museum's holdings. One such purchase was the Barbarigo gallery, a collection begun in the sixteenth century when Titian's son Pomponio sold his deceased father's paintings to the Venetian patrician Christoforo Barbarigo. The collection was acquired for the Hermitage in 1850 by Alexander Khvostov, the Russian consul in Venice, at a cost of 525,000 francs. Contemporaries observed that the gallery contained many mediocre works; as nineteenth-century poet and critic Piotr Viazaemsky asserted, "The sale of the Barbarigo gallery to the Russian court is an unprecedented act of theft." But any shortcomings were easily outweighed by the addition to the Hermitage of its finest works by Titian: *The Repentant Mary Magdalene* and *Saint Sebastian*.

Another highly significant acquisition, made the same year, was a group of paintings from the collection of Nicholas I's son-in-law, King William II of the Netherlands, who died on March 17, 1849. Sent to Holland for the auction, Bruni managed to choose successfully. Of the outstanding works he purchased, particular mention should be made of the masterpieces by Jan van Eyck (*The Annunciation*, now in the National Gallery in Washington, D.C.) and Rogier van der Weyden (half of *St. Luke Drawing the Virgin*, the other half of which was bought in Alexander III's reign), as well as Sebastiano del Piombo's *Lamentation* and Francesco Melzi's *Flora* (long attributed to Leonardo da Vinci). In the spring of 1852 Bruni was again dispatched abroad, this time to Paris, for the sale of Marshal Soult's collection. His purchases this time enriched the Hermitage with additional works by

RIGHT

The Gallery of the History of Ancient Painting in the New Hermitage. Architect: Leo von Klenze, with the participation of Vasily Stasov and Nicolas Yefimov, 1851.

The superb collection of sculptures by Canova and Thorvaldsen now housed in this gallery fully accords with its Neoclassical program, which succinctly expresses the concept of all Nicholas I's Hermitage: ancient and modern artists placed side by side, beneath the canopy of the unshakeable ideal of beauty.

Spanish artists, including Zurbarán's *St. Lawrence* and *The Liberation of the Apostle Peter from the Dungeon* by Murillo, whose paintings were tremendously popular at the time. Bruni failed, however, to secure Murillo's *Immaculate Conception* (now in the Louvre) because its astronomical price tag of 586,000 francs exceeded the funds allotted to him.

Russian collectors also contributed to the growth of the Hermitage. In 1843, the diplomat Dmitry Tatishchev bequeathed to Nicholas I a collection that included works of early Netherlandish painting (Robert Campin's *Virgin and Child by the Fireplace* and Jan Provost's *Virgin and Child*) and cameos stored in a portable chest made by Johann Volkmann. In 1851 a collection of ancient sculpture was bought from the Demidovs, a family of prominent early industrialists. It contained more than fifty statues and reliefs that had been excavated in Italy, including a marble statue of Emperor Antoninus Pius found in Rome in 1825. (Nikolai Demidov had financed digs at Tivoli and in Rome, by the Lateran Gate.)

Treasures arrived from native sites as well. Excavations in Kerch, the ancient Panticapaion dubbed "the Russian Pompeii," heralded the coming-of-age of archaeology in Russia, the birth of which had been signalled by the discovery in 1830 of an ancient burial in the Kul-Oba kurgan (tumulus). On the emperor's orders valuable finds were brought to St. Petersburg, where they were included in the collections of the Hermitage's Department of Antiquities.

The Leonardo da Vinci Hall in the Large (Old) Hermitage. Architects: Yuri Veldten, 1780s; Giacomo Quarenghi, 1805–07; Andrei Stakenschneider, 1858.
This hall, now used to display the greatest treasures of the Hermitage's painting collection, has traveled a sort of circle in its 200-plus years of history. In the late 18th century, it housed part of what was then Catherine II's private art collection. Next, the reconstructed hall became part of a set of apartments reserved for distinguished guests staying at the palace. Finally, after the Second World War, it was returned to its museum status. Since then the hall has contained two masterpieces by Leonardo da Vinci and borne the great Italian artist's name.

Although the Imperial Archaeological Commission was established only in 1859, during the reign of Alexander II, to a large extent we owe its creation to Nicholas I and his genuine interest in archaeological studies, which thus benefited from patronage at the highest level of the state. Nicholas personally visited excavations on several occasions, notably at Kerch in the autumn of 1837. While he was there, Anton Ashik, the director of the local museum, respectfully showed the emperor a recently discovered burial known as the tomb of Rhescuporis. The articles found there, including a silver dish with a Greek inscription featuring the name of King Rhescuporis of Cimmerian Bosporus and a gold burial mask, are still in the Hermitage today. During Nicholas's trip to Italy in 1845, excavations were organized specially for him at Pompeii, and the King of Naples presented the artifacts found to his august guest. Among these were the marble *Boy with a Bird* and a miniature bronze bust of the young Caligula that served as a weight for hand-held scales.

Under Nicholas the practice of buying ancient sculpture in Italy was revived, and a Russian commission was established in Rome to seek out antiquities. The year 1834 was marked by the purchase from the physician and surgeon Pizzati of a collection of antiquities that included more than a thousand painted vases, with several masterpieces among them, especially works by the ancient Greek craftsmen Exekias and "the Amasis painter" (sixth century BC); until the construction of the New Hermitage, this collection was kept in the Academy of Arts and then transferred to the new imperial museum. In 1851 the Hermitage obtained a number of ancient sculptures, including *A Resting Satyr* and *Cupid Drawing His Bow*, in exchange for allowing the pope to retain a plot of land on the Palatine Hill that had earlier been acquired with the intention of excavating there. And in 1852 Nicholas acquired some three hundred ancient vases and more than fifty sculptures from the daughters of the collection's creators, Count Ivan Stepanovich and Countess Alexandra Grigoryevna de la Valle. This acquisition brought to the Hermitage notable marble portraits of Gaius Julius Caesar and Emperor Balbinus.

The course of time and the growth of the collections brought changes to the original layout of Nicholas I's museum. Although no new rooms were added, collections were moved as necessary, such as in 1897 when the canvases in the fore-hall and adjoining Hall of the Russian School were transferred to the Russian Museum. (A Department of Russian Culture appeared in the Hermitage only in Soviet times.) Earlier, during the reign of Alexander II (r. 1855–81), the son of the museum's creator, the Hall of Cameos became the Hall of Majolica; the second glyptic hall is now known as the Knights' Hall; and cameos from the modern era are today displayed in the Golden Drawing Room of the Winter Palace and adjoining Green Dining Room. The fore-hall now holds works by Flemish painters that initially adorned one of the New Hermitage's Skylight Halls. The halls that contained manuscripts, prints, and drawings were taken over by ancient sculpture, and modern sculpture was moved to the landing of the main staircase and the Gallery of the History of Ancient Painting.

Like his predecessors, Alexander engaged in acquisitions as well, including the 1861 purchase of part of the collection of Giovanni Pietro Campana, Marchese di Cavelli (1809–1880). This unusual collector, who conducted his own excavations and energetically bought old paintings, inherited the small assemblage of antiquities bequeathed to him by his grandfather, archaeologist Giampietro Campana, and transformed it into a truly grand collection. The marchese's impulsive nature led to the collapse of his career; in 1857 he was arrested and brought to trial for embezzling public funds. Upon conviction his property was confiscated, and his collection of more than nine thousand items, including some four thousand ancient painted vases and over five hundred statues, was put up for sale.

It was thanks to Campana's passion for antiquities that the Hermitage came into possession of an extremely large number of Greek and Italian vases. "After absorbing the enormous Campana collection," remarked Russian man of letters Dmitry Grigorovich, "the Hermitage museum suddenly acquired European significance." From the disgraced nobleman's collection, Stepan Gedeonov, head of the commission seeking out antiquities (and, from 1863, first director of the Hermitage), selected 78 sculptures, 193 bronzes, some 500 painted vases, and 9 frescoes by Raphael's studio. The most curious item was a colossal marble statue of Jupiter (measuring 3.57 meters tall and weighing 16 tons), which had been found at Castel Gandolfo in 1780, among the ruins of Emperor Domitian's villa, and reassembled by sculptor Vincenzo Pacetti. (This same sculpture, derived from a masterpiece by Phidias, had once been offered to Catherine the Great.) Another notable item was the "Cumae Vase," a black-glazed hydria (water vessel) whose relief decoration was made from clay pressed in molds, which was then painted and gilded. The so-called Queen of Vases was much admired, as attested by French archaeologist Raoul Rochette, who exclaimed: "It is a wonder of which I do not know the like!" It also elicited no small amount of jealousy, as evidenced in the words of French politician and writer Ludovic Vitet, who believed that France should purchase the entire collection: "Russia stole not only the Cumae vase, that 'queen of vases,' and twenty more in the same style, but a further 35 vases of colossal size from Ruvo." The coveted vase, along with the other acquisitions from the Campana collection, was delivered to St. Petersburg in 1862, necessitating further changes to the museum's interior organization. The library that had been part of Nicholas I's museum, together with the manuscripts, was transferred to the Public Library (today the National Library of Russia), and the ground-floor rooms were arranged to accommodate the fresh arrivals. Meanwhile, the School of Raphael frescoes depicting subjects from Ovid's *Metamorphoses* (*The Abduction of Helen*, *Venus and Cupid*, and the like), which had formerly adorned the Villa Spada on the Palatine Hill in Rome, were set into the walls of the Empress's Cabinet on the upper floor.

During Gedeonov's tenure as museum director, several outstanding works were purchased in Italy. From the collection of Count Antonio Litta, owner of the family gallery in Milan, Gedeonov selected a few works in 1864, including a *Madonna and Child* by Leonardo da Vinci that has since borne the name of its former owner: the *Litta Madonna*. Five years later the owner of another long-established collection, Count Conestabile, proposed to sell to the Hermitage a picture gallery and a small assortment of drawings. After prolonged negotiations (and a wave of public protest in Italy due to the government's inability to raise its own acquisition funds), a Raphael *Madonna* was purchased for 310,000 francs; Alexander II subsequently presented it as a gift to his wife, Maria Fiodorovna. Like Leonardo's masterpiece, this work is known today by the name of its former owner: the *Conestabile Madonna*.

The reign of Alexander III (1881–94), who assumed the throne after the assassination of his father on March 1, brought unprecedented activity in the formation of the Hermitage's collections of applied art and the beginning of the systematic study of the artistic crafts. Hitherto the emphasis in this area had been on decorative rather than historical aspects; in the second half of the nineteenth century, however, with the art industry developing apace, applied art became a specialized field of collecting. In 1870 the Society for the Encouragement of the Arts had created a Museum of Applied Art, and in 1884 Alexander Polovtsov established a museum attached to the Baron Stieglitz Central College of Technical Drawing, both in St. Petersburg. (After the October Revolution of 1917 the stocks of both institutions entered the Hermitage.) In 1885 Alexander III acquired an important collection of ancient applied art consisting of Tanagra terracotta figurines, which had been assembled in Greece by Count Piotr Saburov, a diplomat. The works had caused a sensation at the 1878 world's fair in Paris, and in the 1880s a sumptuous catalogue compiled by German archaeologist Adolf Furtwängler was published in Berlin. Several museums vied for the privilege of acquiring works from Saburov's collection, and indeed the count's marble sculptures were sold to Berlin and the bronzes to London. Yet the Hermitage succeeded in securing the celebrated figurines. As Saburov wrote to Prince Alexander Vasilchikov, then director of the Hermitage: "Don't regret my marbles. . . . Your Kerch hall combined with my Tanagras will surpass . . . all museums in the world. Evidently this coming winter they will be the stars of the St. Petersburg season."

Perhaps the most significant acquisition by Alexander III, however, was the collection of the Paris-based diplomat Alexander Bazilevsky (1829–1899). Assembled with a precise aim—to show the formation of Christian art in Europe between the third and the fourteenth century—the collection was exhibited in its own hall in the Palais de Trocadéro at the 1878 world's exhibition in Paris. Connoisseurs and the general public alike hailed the new Parisian collection: "This astonishing hall of Monsieur Bazilevsky's cannot be compared with anything. . . . What splendor! Carved ivory, jewellery, manuscripts, weaponry, painted enamels, Palissy ceramics. In short, there is everything here that the artistic crafts produced from the start of the Middle Ages to the end of the sixteenth century." Grand Duke Alexander, then heir to the Russian throne, had viewed the works at Bazilevsky's mansion on the Rue Blanche, as noted by the artist Alexei Bogomolov, who wrote to his colleague Mikhail Botkin in St. Petersburg: "He visited Bazilevsky's collection in Paris with me accompanying him and that was when it occurred to him to buy it for Russia." Another person in favor of acquiring the entire collection was secretary of state Alexander Polovtsov, who, early in 1884, wrote of his intentions: "I propose acquiring also Bazilevsky's collection . . . adding to it the best pieces from the Tsarskoye Selo Arsenal and installing all of it in the large, well-lit halls where the cases of medals stand now." In the autumn of 1884 Polovtsov informed Alexander, now tsar: "I have received a letter from Bogolyubov in Paris. [In his opinion] if the collection is not bought in the

course of November, then from December 1 Bazilevsky will be in the clutches of the expert Mannheim and we will not get the collection under any circumstances." From his own funds, Alexander paid nearly 5.5 million francs (about 2.2 million gold rubles) for 762 items. The press trumpeted the extraordinary event, and Polovtsov too celebrated, as recorded in his diary: "We dropped into the Hermitage to look at Bazilevsky's collection. I could not be more delighted to have aided in its acquisition. Such objects do not exist in Russia, and until now they have been accessible only to those of our compatriots who had the money to travel. Now they can be seen by the least artisan."

With this acquisition it was now possible to organize in the museum a new Department of the Middle Ages and Renaissance. The display was created in the ground-floor suite of the Old Hermitage, which had been used by the State Council until its move to the Mariinsky Palace. The collection of Western European artistic arms and armor from the fifteenth to the seventeenth century, begun by Alexander I (who had a great interest in the history of knighthood), was considerably enlarged through purchases made in Europe. The collection contained unique works by the master armorers of Italy, Germany, Spain, and France. Further augmenting the New Hermitage's stores were the collections transferred in 1885 from the Tsarskoye Selo Arsenal, including a large stock of Russian weaponry as well as a splendid Eastern collection, the core of which was trophies and diplomatic gifts from the time of Russia's Persian, Turkish, central Asian, and Caucasian wars. The Hermitage grew again in 1886 when the collection of the Princes Golitsyn was bought in Moscow; several collections of Thracian and Macedonian antiquities formed during the Russo-Turkish War of 1877–78 and the surviving bronze ornaments of a Thracian chariot found by the Russian consul Naiden Gerov in the Dukhova Mogila burial mound in Bulgaria added still more to its many treasures.

Edward Hau. The Cabinet of the Italian Schools in the New Hermitage. 1856. Watercolor on paper.
11 ¾ x 11 ¼ in. (29.8 x 28.6 cm).
In the second row on the right, by the door, is Titian's Venus with a Mirror, *which was sold in 1931 to Andrew Mellon, the financier and U.S. Treasury Secretary, and later became part of the collection of the National Gallery that he founded in Washington, D.C. In the 19th century, the painting was such an undisputed masterpiece that a copy could be placed in the same room, on the other side of the door.*

The advent of the twentieth century brought many significant changes to the Hermitage, and to Russia as a whole. Although the reign of Nicholas II (r. 1894–1917) is almost unanimously considered to be a period of stagnation in the museum's affairs, a number of important events must be noted. First, in 1910 the museum absorbed a unique collection of Dutch paintings put together by the scholar and statesman Piotr Semionov-Tian-Shansky, who aimed to supplement the Hermitage's stocks in areas that were lacking. Semionov-Tian-Shansky, a geographer and ethnographer, became a considerable expert in his chosen field of collecting, publishing *Studies in the History of Netherlandish Painting* in 1885. Thanks to his efforts, in 1886 the Hermitage recovered the wings of Lucas van Leyden's altarpiece *The Healing of the Blind Man of*

Jericho, which had been sold at auction in 1854. The scholar's collection, purchased at half its actual price, was left at his disposal during his lifetime and came into the museum only in 1915, after his death and a memorial exhibition held in 1914. The collection numbered more than seven hundred paintings, most notably works by artists previously unrepresented in the Hermitage, such as members of Rembrandt's immediate circle. It added still lifes by Willem Kalf and François Ryckhals, landscapes by Salomon van Ruysdael and Jan van Goyen, Abraham van den Tempel's *Portrait of a Widow*, David Teniers the Younger's *Landscape with a Rainbow*, and much more.

In 1912, the Hermitage's holdings of English works was supplemented by the collection of Alexei Khitrovo, Master of the Imperial Court Hunt. It included all the finest examples of eighteenth-century English portraits now displayed in the museum: works by Gainsborough, Romney, Lawrence, Raeburn, and others. Two years later the museum acquired another painting by Leonardo da Vinci, the *Benois Madonna*, purchased from Maria Benois, wife of court architect Leonty Benois. (Leonardo's authorship was established by Ernst Liphart, the chief curator of the Hermitage picture gallery.)

The year 1914 saw the outbreak of the First World War, and with it preparations began for the evacuation of the Hermitage's greatest treasures to Moscow. There, the crated exhibits were stored in the Kremlin Palace, the Historical Museum, and the Museum of Fine Arts. As the war intensified, the Winter Palace was used as a hospital for wounded soldiers, who were treated in the sumptuous state rooms—the Nicholas and Armorial Halls—a conversion that was personally overseen by Empress Alexandra Fiodorovna. When German forces approached Riga, the time had come to evacuate the stocks still remaining in Petrograd (as St. Petersburg had been renamed in August 1914 in a reaction against the city's Germanic name). But circumstances prevented further removal of works: The revolutionary year of 1917 had begun.

As part of the imperial court, the Hermitage was strongly affected by the political upheavals raging both at home and abroad. Although at first the museum staff boycotted the new Bolshevik authorities, soon they obeyed the orders of the official, appointed to the Hermitage by Anatoly Lunacharsky, People's Commissar for Education. In October the Winter Palace was declared "a state museum on a par with the Hermitage" and renamed the Palace of Arts; Palace Square was given the name Moisei Uritsky, after the head of the Petrograd Cheka who was assassinated there. Soon after the revolution of 1917, the state rooms of the Winter Palace were opened to the public for lectures, films, and concerts. The first exhibitions opened in the Hermitage in 1919, and by November 1920, albeit with much difficulty, the museum recovered all the masterpieces that had been evacuated to Moscow. Meanwhile, in the 1920s the Hermitage's stocks as much as doubled as the process of nationalizing private and palace collections contributed to its holdings of artworks and valuables from imperial residences and palaces of the Russian nobility.

Sadly, the Hermitage lost several outstanding specialists during this time, many never to return. The prerevolutionary director of the Hermitage, Count Dmitry Tolstoi, had left Russia, going first to the Ukraine and then settling in France. As early as 1920 a purge was conducted of museum staff on the basis of social class (targeting members of the White Guard, officers of the Tsarist Army, former factory owners, nobles, hereditary, and honorary citizens deemed to be "clogging the apparatus"). In conjunction with the dismissal of personnel came the loss of exceptional artworks through a series of sales, the scale of which was long hidden under a veil of silence. Beginning in the winter of 1919, Soviet authorities appointed an "expert commission," chaired by the writer Maxim Gorky, to select works in Petrograd suitable for sale. With the aim (or pretext) of helping the state's starving population, mass confiscation of valuables was carried out, particularly from churches and monasteries. Treasures from the Romanov family collection were made available for viewing and then for purchase by foreign buyers, dispersing them far and wide: Presentation Easter eggs made by the craftsmen of the House of Fabergé later passed into the hands of the Forbes publishing family in New York; a mosaic egg with portraits of the last imperial couple's five children now graces the collection of Queen Elizabeth II; and the diamond-studded "wedding crown" eventually ended up in the collection of Marjorie Merriweather Post, the former wife of U.S. ambassador to Moscow Joseph E. Davies. On March 16, 1927, Christie's in London held an auction of items from the USSR Diamond Fund.

The massive sales of works from the Hermitage collections continued into the 1930s and 1940s. One of the main commercial partners of the new Soviet government was the American physician and businessman Armand Hammer (1898–1990), who had traveled to the Soviet Union in 1921 to help with famines and disease plaguing the country and ended up staying nine years. In his 1932 book *The Quest of the Romanoff Treasure*, Hammer described the history of his collection like a detective story. The collector's first meeting with Lenin, so he claimed, was a confidential chat: "Russia today is like your country was during the pioneer stage," the head of the Bolshevik government told him. "What we really need [. . .] is American capital and technical aid to get our wheels turning once more . . . Why don't you take an asbestos concession yourself?" That was how Lenin ended his conversation with the American doctor who had brought grain and medicines for the starving and typhoid victims in the Urals.

Soon the American tycoon began buying paintings. When he dared to advise Anastas Mikoyan, the head of the People's Commissariat for Foreign Trade, to stop removing masterpieces from the museums so that the West would not form the impression that the Soviet economy was bankrupt, he was supposedly told: "You can have the Old Masters for the moment. But we are right now preparing a revolution in your country, and we will get them back." Another of the Soviet leadership's partners in the sale of museum treasures who received a similar warning from Mikoyan was the oil magnate

Calouste Gulbenkian, head of the transnational Iraq Petroleum Company. Among his most valuable acquisitions were Houdon's statue *Diana* and the Rembrandt masterpieces *Portrait of an Old Man* and *Alexander the Great* (all three now in the Museu Calouste Gulbenkian in Lisbon) as well as views of the park at Versailles by Hubert Robert, *Portrait of Helena Fourment* by Rubens, and an *Annunciation* by Dirck Bouts. To repay Soviet Russia for the opportunity to make such acquisitions, Gulbenkian acted as an intermediary in oil deals.

The most valuable acquisition—and the greatest loss for the Hermitage—was probably made by U.S. Treasury Secretary Andrew Mellon (1855–1937). In September 1928 the Hermitage received from Moscow a "Special list of paintings to be transferred to Antikvariat" (the organization set up to export and import antiques and art). It consisted exclusively of world-ranking masterpieces, the majority of which were later sold to Mellon: 1) Botticelli, *Adoration of the Magi*; 2) Raphael, *Alba Madonna*; 3) Caravaggio, *Madonna*; 4) Giorgione, *Judith*; 5) Tiepolo, *Cleopatra's Feast*; 6) Rogier van der Weyden, *St. Luke Painting the Virgin*; 7) Dirck Bouts, *Annunciation*; 8) Rembrandt, *Young Woman with Flowers*; 9–10) Rembrandt, *Pallas Athena* and *Girl with a Broom*; 11–12) Rembrandt, *Portrait of an Old Man* and *Portrait of Titus*; 13) Rubens, *Portrait of an Elderly Woman*; 14–15) Rubens, *Perseus and Andromeda* and *Portrait of Helena Fourment*; 16) Rubens, *Landscape with a Rainbow*; 17) Rubens, *Landscape with Stone-Haulers*; 18) Watteau, *Jester Playing a Lute*; 19) Watteau, *An Embarrassing Proposal*; 20) Jan van Eyck, *Annunciation*; and 21) Fragonard, *The Stolen Kiss*. At a meeting in the Hermitage Dmitry Shmidt, head of the Picture Gallery, suggested ceding at most five paintings whose loss would be the least catastrophic—numbers 7, 8, 11, 13, and 19— placing on them a value of 650,000 pounds sterling. He ended his address with these words: "The removal of any five paintings on the said list will cause immense harm to the main collections of the Hermitage. . . . From all that has been said, it follows that the Hermitage cannot part with a single one of the paintings listed."

What weight did the lamentations of an expert carry? Apparently very little, for the authorities had no intention of limiting themselves to five canvases. In the end, thirteen works from the list had to leave the Hermitage, and, to add insult to injury, more works were added: four van Dycks (portraits of Lord Wharton, Isabella Brant, an unknown woman, and Susanna Fourment with her daughter); *Portrait of Pope Innocent X* by Velázquez; *Portrait of a Polish Aristocrat* and *Portrait of an Eastern Man* by Rembrandt; Titian's *Venus before the Mirror*; a *Crucifixion* triptych by Perugino; two portraits by Frans Hals; Chardin's *House of Cards*; *St. George* by Raphael; *Moses Found* by Veronese; and Adriaen Hanneman's *Portrait of the Duke of Gloucester*. The collection of Old Master paintings that Mellon accumulated by the mid-1930s was valued at $35 million, though he had expended just over $6 million to acquire them. His most expensive acquisition was Raphael's celebrated tondo, the *Alba Madonna*, for which he paid just over $1.1 million. Shortly before his death, in December 1936, Mellon announced in a letter to President Roosevelt that he was presenting the National Gallery, which he had founded in Washington D.C. and stocked with treasures from the Hermitage, to the American people.

In the postrevolutionary period, the Hermitage's exhibitions began to be organized in keeping with Marxist ideology. As evidence, it is enough to quote some of the display titles: "The Petit-Bourgeois Art of the Pre-Revolutionary Period in the Low Countries," "French Art from the Period of the Decay of Feudalism and the Bourgeois Revolution," and the like. Beginning in 1925, a new type of museum display was developed and the role and significance of art were reassessed. Ancient artifacts or Old Master paintings, for example, were now understood not simply as valuable masterpieces—objects of abstract aesthetic admiration—but as historical documents and material evidence of specific eras, as reflections and embodiments of the ideologies of various social groupings and successive social orders. Although at times overly simplistic, the sociological method did produce interesting results, especially in the presentation of archaeological material, whose displays often included craftwork accompanied by tools and everyday objects, helping to create a more rounded historical context. Subordinated to the Bolsheviks' declared aim of enlightening the masses, these methods coincided in many ways with the most advanced display techniques being introduced in museums throughout Europe and the United States. When visiting Berlin in 1925, Oscar Waldhauer

The architectural complex of the Hermitage, within the ensemble of St. Petersburg's city center.

(chair of the Committee for the Sociological Study of Art at the State Institute for the History of the Arts) observed that "it is amusing that these people, anything but Marxists, adhere to Marxist principles when organizing exhibitions. The advance of learning has produced this and they cannot do otherwise." The success of the sociological method, as applied to the display of ancient cultural artifacts, furthered archaeological activity on the part of the Hermitage as well.

The Second World War brought unprecedented trials to the Hermitage, endangering not only its collections and architecture but its staff as well. Thanks to measures taken in advance, the museum's masterpieces were evacuated to the safety of Sverdlovsk, in the Urals. Civil-defense units were formed to protect the museum complex, and twelve bomb shelters were created in its cellars, within which some two thousand people lived. Staff members took turns guarding the museum and performing defensive work, digging anti-tank ditches and the like. Many joined the ranks of the Red Army (six dying at the front), and another forty-three perished in the city during the nine-hundred-day siege of Leningrad. One touching piece of oral history about the beleaguered Hermitage recounts how one of the museum's best guides, a man named Pavel Gubchevsky, presented a moving tour around the empty halls to soldiers who had arrived to clear away broken glass from the explosions. During the darkest days of the siege, when those living in the museum cellars were forced to collect water from holes cut into the ice on the Neva, the Hermitage stood proud, a testament to the strength and perseverance of the Russian people.

On January 18, 1944, staff and citizens alike were at last given a cause for celebration with the lifting of the siege, and preparations soon began for the exhibition "Works of Culture and Art That Remained in Leningrad During the Siege," scheduled for November 7. By the end of June 1945, nearly thirty thousand people had visited the exhibition. But the true celebration took place on May 9, 1945, when the entire country rejoiced in the victory over Nazi Germany. Amid the celebrations, the Hermitage was pressing ahead with preparations for a large exhibition showcasing the treasures returned from the Urals.

Despite the sad losses suffered during the postrevolutionary period and the honorably borne hardships of two world wars and years of civil unrest, the Hermitage never ceased growing. New departments have been created, including that of the History of Russian Culture in 1941, and additional structures have been incorporated into the museum, such as, in 1981, the Menshikov Palace on Vasilyevsky Island in St. Petersburg, which houses the exhibition "The Culture of Russia in the First Third of the 18th Century." Repairs to the Hermitage buildings have also revealed fascinating details about the complex's early history. When work was conducted on the Hermitage Theater in 1992, it was discovered that Peter the Great's Winter Palace had not been completely razed when Giacomo Quarenghi erected the new theater on the site, as had previously been thought; the architect had retained not only some of the palace's basement and ground-floor walls but also entire groups of rooms. As a result, present-day restoration architects have managed to add one more section to the displays relating to Peter's time. Most recently, the Hermitage museum complex was joined by the left side of the General Staff building, across Palace Square, an outstanding work by the architect Carlo Rossi. This addition gives the museum the opportunity to organize immense displays. One of the first, "Realms of the Eagle: The Empire Style," opened in 1999 in rooms that were once the apartment of the Minister of Foreign Affairs. The exhibits were complemented well by the interiors designed by Rossi in the 1820s, and visitors were able to see works of applied art that usually remain out of sight in the Hermitage storerooms: magnificent decorative bronzes, furniture, silver, porcelain, fabrics, and costumes from the glittering Empire era. The museum in the General Staff building became the Hermitage's second branch, after the Menshikov Palace. It is planned that this structure will house a new suite of exhibition halls, restoration services, storerooms, and research rooms, all fitted with state-of-the-art equipment.

Today's Hermitage—not just a museum but a global cultural and research complex—remains true to its centuries-old tradition. In 2003, during the celebrations of St. Petersburg's Tercentenary, the main entrance to the complex, through the Great Courtyard of the Winter Palace, was reopened. Now all visitors, just like the aristocratic elite of the eighteenth century and the official delegations of the present day, approach the museum from Palace Square, passing through the triple arch adorned with superbly restored gates that pierce the palace's south wing. The grand courtyard has become an organic part of the museum complex. It is the first thing that greets visitors as they enter the chief residence of the Russian monarchs, extraordinary rulers who demonstrated their country's openness to all cultures by gathering together one of the largest, richest, most encyclopedic collections of the world's treasures.

Ancient Egyptian, Near Eastern, and Asian Art

Throne Ornament in the Form of a Sphinx. Urartu. 7th century B.C. Bronze with traces of gilding, inlaid white stone.
6 ¼ in. (16 cm) high.
The hollow figurine of a winged lion with a human torso and head crowned with a tiara once adorned a throne in a
palace or temple. It is unique, made in an expensive and laborious technique that allowed only a single cast from a wax
model. It was originally covered with extremely thin gold foil, and the grooves on the wings were filled with a red paste.

The Stela of Ipi. New Kingdom, Ancient
Egypt. Second half of the 14th century
B.C. (18th dynasty). Limestone.
37 ⅜ x 28 in. (95 x 71 cm).
Ipi was a high-ranking official, the royal
scribe and fan-bearer to Tutankhamun.
That pharaoh's reign was marked by a
reaction to the religious reforms of his
predecessor, Amenhotep IV (Akhenaton),
and the resumption of worship of the
ancient gods. Depictions of these begin to
appear again on objects in the tombs of
private individuals. This stela, showing Ipi
praying before the god Anubis, is among
the earliest artifacts of that type.

Statue of Amenemhat III. Middle
Kingdom, Ancient Egypt. Late 19th–early
18th century B.C. Black granite (diorite).
35 in. (86.5 cm) high.
The reign of the pharaoh Amenemhat III
Nymare was marked by military successes
and economic prosperity, accompanied
by large-scale construction. This statue is
a superb example of the realistic royal
portrait common in ancient Egypt.
Amenemhat is dressed in a pleated skirt
and wears a *nemes*, the royal headcloth.
The indentations at the temple were
made to attach a false beard, another
attribute of supreme power.

Statue of the Scribe Maniamon. New Kingdom, Ancient Egypt. Second half of the 15th century B.C. (18th dynasty). Limestone. 14 ⅞ in. (37.6 cm) high.

This statue of a scribe who tallied grain in the Temple of Karnak belongs to the cuboid type. The clothing is tightly stretched by the squatting figure with arms crossed over the knees, turning it into a cubic volume. In keeping with New Kingdom practice, the official's features resemble those of the reigning pharaoh, in this case Amenhotep II. The carved hieroglyphic inscription contains the usual text of a prayer to Amon-Ra and Osiris.

Statue of the Goddess Mut-Sekhmet. New Kingdom, Ancient Egypt. First half of the 14th century B.C. (18th dynasty). Granite. 78 ¾ in. (200 cm) high.

This monumental temple statue of the lion-headed Mut-Sekhmet was bought at Thebes in 1835 by the scholar and writer Avraam Norov. He wrote that an Egyptian noblewoman asked permission to board the boat on which the statue was being transported, "looked long at it in great pensiveness, then knelt down, piously kissed its breast and went away with tears in her eyes." This astonishing event is vivid proof of the survival in Muslim Egypt of vestiges of the ancient cult.

Statue of Queen Cleopatra VII. 51–33 B.C.
Black basalt. 41 ⅜ in. (105 cm) high.
This statue conforms to the traditional
Egyptian canon and is one of the best
sculptural depictions of a ruler of
Ptolemaic Egypt, in terms of
workmanship and state of preservation.
In the figure's right hand is an ankh,
Egyptian symbol of life, and in her left
is a horn of plenty, an attribute adopted
from Greece. The three uraei (sacred
asps) in the wig are specific to depictions
of Cleopatra VII, while the cornucopia
also occurs in statues of earlier rulers.

Isis with Horus. Late Period, Ancient
Egypt. 7th–6th century B.C. (26th
dynasty). Cast bronze. 15 in. (38 cm).
The goddess Isis—protectress of magic,
wife of the god Osiris, and mother of the
god Horus—always occupied an
important place in the Egyptians'
mythology and religion but apparently
did not have her own cult. In Hellenistic
and Roman times, by contrast, her cult
became widespread. She can be
unerringly identified by her
characteristic attribute: cow's horns, with
a sun disk between them. The image
of Isis suckling the infant Horus,
common in small-scale Egyptian art
of the late periods, subsequently
influenced Christian iconography.

Statuette of a Priest. New Kingdom,
Ancient Egypt. Mid-14th century B.C.
(18th dynasty). Wood.
13 ½ in. (34.5 cm) high.
The youthful face of the priest with
slanting almond-shaped eyes finds close
parallels in the portraits created of the
pharaoh Amenhotep III in the last years
of his reign. At the same time the
plumpness of the belly and chest, which
in ancient Egyptian art indicates age,
suggests that the man depicted was not
young at all. His shaven head is evidence
that he held high priestly rank.

The Stela of Horemheb. New Kingdom, Ancient Egypt. Late 14th–early 13th century B.C. (18th dynasty). Limestone. 30 ¾ x 42 ¾ in. (78 x 108.6 cm). While still commander in chief of the army, the future pharaoh and founder of the 19th dynasty began to construct a magnificent tomb for himself at Saqqara, near Memphis. On this stela, which was part of its interior decoration, Horemheb is depicted praying to the gods Atum, Osiris, and Ptah-Seker. Since the Saqqara tomb was constructed before Horemheb's ascent to the throne, his likeness does not include the uraeus, an attribute of kingship.

LEFT

Ptah and Sekhmet. Late Period, Ancient Egypt. 7th–6th century B.C. (26th dynasty). Basalt. 22 ⅞ in. (58 cm) high.

Ptah—the chief deity of Memphis, Egypt's earliest capital—is depicted with his traditional headdress, long tight-fitting clothing, and staff. The figure of his divine spouse, the lion-headed Sekhmet, was carved on a slightly lesser scale. Above her head are the sun disk and a uraeus. The proportions of the figures and the treatment of the details are characteristic of works from the Saite period (663–524 B.C.), whose creators took inspiration from classic prototypes of the era of the great pharaohs.

OPPOSITE

Portrait of a Young Woman. Fayum, Egypt. First half of the 2nd century. Encaustic paint on panel. 12 ⅝ x 5 ⅜ in. (32.2 x 13.5 cm).

The practice of making burial portraits like this, to be placed over the face of a mummy and within the wrappings, arose in Egypt in Roman times, in the first century A.D., uniting features of ancient Egyptian and Greco-Roman traditions. In accordance with the canon, the woman's face, though painted in fine detail, represents an ideal type and lacks strong individuality.

Warriors. Fragment of a relief panel from Kalhu (Nimrud). Third quarter of the 8th century B.C. Limestone. 32 ¼ x 30 ⅜ in. (82 x 77 cm).

The construction of ever-new grand residences that accorded with the growing ambitions of the victorious Assyrian rulers provided sculptors with extensive scope. The multitiered relief friezes that adorned the royal state rooms presented narrative cycles detailing the twists and turns of military campaigns, sieges of enemy fortresses, and scenes of captives being driven off. This relief, for the palace of Tiglath-Pileser III (r. 745–727 B.C.) in Kalhu, is only a small fragment of one such epic glorifying the king's victories and conquests.

A Priest with a Pomegranate Branch. Fragment of a relief panel from Dur-Sharrukin (Khorsabad). Last quarter of the 8th century B.C. Limestone. 41 ¾ x 18 ⅛ in. (106 x 46 cm).

As early as the 9th century B.C., a strict iconographic canon was established in Assyrian art that stressed might, physical strength, and health. Those characteristics find expression in the figures' overdeveloped musculature and luxuriant, thick, curly hair. The ideal of beauty and fortitude leaves no room for individualization; the person's status was indicated by their clothing and attributes. This relief, from the palace of Sargon II (r. 722–705 B.C.) in Dur-Sharrukin, has retained traces of the polychrome painting lost on most artifacts.

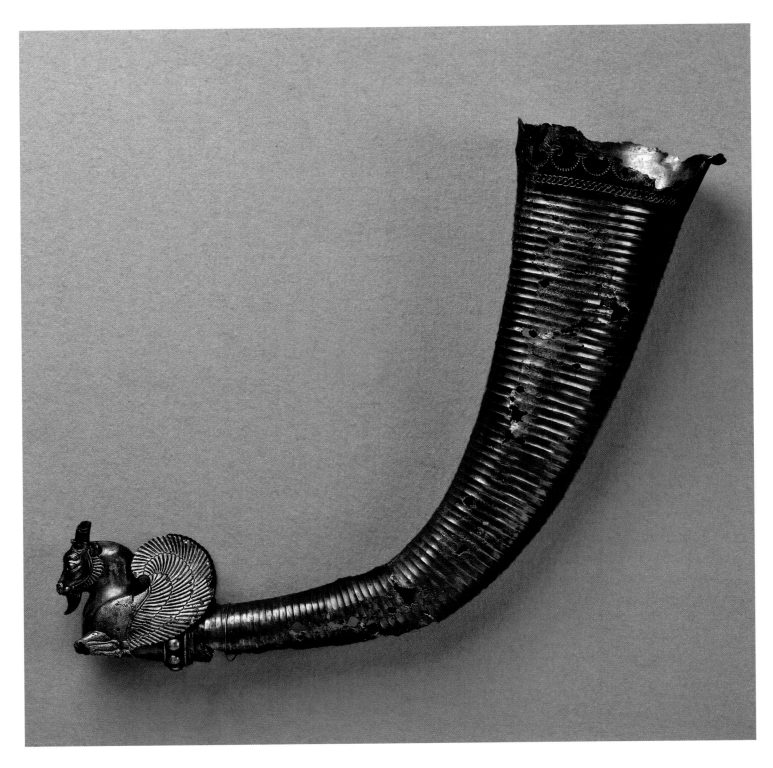

Rhyton with the Half-Figure of a Winged Goat. Iran. Found in the Seven Brothers burial mound, Taman peninsula,
Russia. 5th century B.C. Silver. 24 ⅞ in. (63 cm) external length.
The fantastic winged goat or ibex that adorns this fine drinking vessel is a representation of Veretragna, the Iranian
god of victory. The animal's legs are tucked up, like those of the bulls on the capitals in the Achaemenid palaces
of Persepolis and Susa. The carefully worked hair and feathers are emphatically decorative. Vessels like this, made
of precious metals and incorporating half-figures of mythological animals (such as a winged ibex or a horned gryphon),
probably served a ceremonial function.

OPPOSITE
Wine Jug Bearing a Depiction of a Senmurv. 6th–early 7th century. Gilded silver. 13 in. (33 cm) diameter.
The fantastic *senmurv-paskuj*—the dog-bird of Iranian mythology—was perhaps an emblem of the shahs.
The creature was depicted not only on silver vessels and dishes but also on stone reliefs, seals, fabrics,
and the headdresses of the Sassanid princes.

Dish: King Peroz Hunting. Second half of the 5th century. Gilded silver. 9 ⅝ in. (24.6 cm) diameter.
The silver dishes of Sassanid Iran are official portraits of great nobles and members of the ruling dynasty. This example shows King Peroz (r. 459–84) hunting wild sheep that have been driven into an enclosure. The netting of the enclosure, with the heads of drivers and hunting dogs peeping over the top, forms a border framing the central scene. The dish was cast using the lost-wax process, a rare technique in Sassanid art.

Bahram Out Hunting. 390s. Gilded silver. 11 in. (28 cm) diameter.
Prince Bahram (Varahran) is hunting boars in brushwood: his sword slashes one animal's mighty withers. In accordance with tradition, the heir to the Sassanid ruler is shown in grand attire, wearing a crown topped with ram's horns in accordance with his status. In Zoroastrian symbolism, the boar stands for the god of victory, Veretragna, from whom the prince's name derives. The image has a symbolic subtext that is concealed by the realistic treatment of the hunting scene.

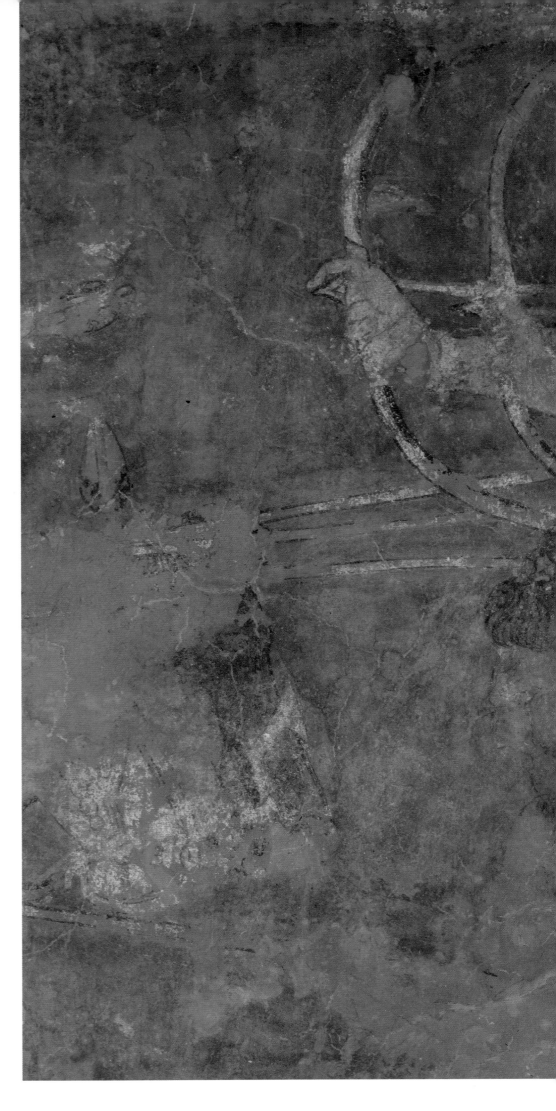

Demons, Enemies of the Hero Rustam.
Detail of the murals in the "Blue Hall."
Pendzhikent, Sogdiana (now Tajikistan).
Ca. 740. Distemper paints on loess
plaster. 39 ⅜ in. (100 cm) high.
The murals excavated at Pendzhikent, an
early medieval city in the valley of the
Zeravshan, represent Sogdianan art at its
peak. In the early-8th century roughly a
third of its dwellings had murals in one or
more rooms. Those in the "Blue Hall"
were ranged in four tiers. The main cycle,
at eye level, depicted the legendary hero
Rustam and his warriors fighting dragons
and demons. The golden figures, painted
in various shades of ochre, stood out
strongly from the ultramarine background
(now much faded). The use of such
expensive paints is evidence of the high
status and wealth of the man who
commissioned the murals.

*The Eleven-Faced Bodhisattva
Avalokitesvara.* 12th century. Khara-
Khoto, Hsi Hsia (a Tangut state in
present-day northwestern China).
Distemper paints on canvas.
52 x 37 in. (132 × 94 cm).
Buddhism—both Tibetan and Chinese—
was an important influence in the
formation of Tangut culture. The
Hermitage *tangka* (religious painting)
depicts the bodhisattva of mercy and
compassion Avalokitesvara, one of the
eight great bodhisattvas, on a lotus throne.
It has eight arms; the two main ones,
placed together in the anjami mudra
gesture, hold the wish-fulfilling jewel.
The central figure is symmetrically
surrounded by other deities of Buddhist
mythology—Buddhas and guardians.
Behind the *mandorla* (radiance) in which
the Avalokitesvara is depicted, two monks
are shown, one young with a grotesque
face, the other old and pleasant-looking.

Portrait of an Official. 12th century.
Khara-Khoto, Hsi Hsia (a Tangut state
in present-day northwestern China).
Distemper paints and India ink on paper.
17 ¾ x 12 ½ in. (45 × 31.8 cm)
A prominent place among the unique
artifacts kept in the Hermitage is reserved
for the artworks of the Tangut, the people
who created the central Asian state of
Hsi Hsia that perished in the Mongol
invasion of 1227. Tangut culture became
known thorough the discoveries made in
1908–9 by Piotr Kozlov's expedition in
the lost fortress of Khara-Khoto (Gobi
Desert, Mongolia). This portrait of
an elderly official, who cannot be
identified due to the lack of any text,
follows the portraiture canon of the
Chinese Sung era.

Scythian and
Bosporan Antiquities

Comb Bearing a Depiction of Battle Scenes. Solokha burial mound, Dnieper river basin, Zaporozhye region, Ukraine. Last third of the 5th–early 4th century B.C. Gold. 5 in. (12.6 cm) high, 4 in. (10.2 cm) wide.

The scene on the back of this gold comb probably illustrates a Scythian legend or myth or perhaps a glorified historical episode: the culmination of the dynastic conflict between the sons of the Scythian king Ariapithes. The shape repeats those made of a combination of metal and bone or wood often found in the burials of the Scythian aristocracy. It is a masterpiece of Greek metalworking made for a Scythian client.

LEFT
Plaque in the Form of a Panther.
Kelermes, Kuban river basin, Krasnodar territory, Russia. 7th–6th century B.C.
Gold. 12 ⅞ in. (32.6 cm) long. This piece was previously believed to have adorned a shield, but a better argument places it on a *gorytos*—a combination of quiver and case for a Scythian bow. The panther's eye, ear, and, originally, nostril were accentuated using colored inlays. Along its tucked-up tail and paws are ten more stylized figures of curled-up predators that served to multiply the object's power.

BELOW
Plaque in the Form of a Deer. Burial mound near the Cossack village of Kostromskaya, Kuban river basin, Krasnodar territory, Russia. Late 7th century B.C. Gold. 12 ½ in. (31.7 cm) long, 7 ½ in. (19 cm) high.
This plaque once embellished a shield or bow case that may have belonged to a member of the elite of the clan's tribal aristocracy. The relief is a true masterpiece of Scythian metalworking and a copybook example of the mature Animal Style. An accurate depiction of the deer is combined with a decorative yet concise treatment of the details; it is shown as if prepared for a ritual sacrifice. Sockets in the eye and ear were originally filled with an inlay, now lost.

OPPOSITE
Plaque in the Form of a Coiled Panther. Southwest Siberia, between the Rivers Irtysh and Ob. 7th–6th century B.C. Gold. 4 ⅜ in. (11 cm), greatest diameter.
This magnificent example of the Scythian Animal Style, relating to the culture of the ancient nomads of the Altai Mountains, comes from the Siberian Collection of Peter the Great. This group of antiquities was assembled between 1715 and 1718 on the tsar's orders by Prince Matvei Gagarin from items that had been plundered from ancient burials. After Peter's death, the collection was long kept in the Kunstkammer, the museum he founded, and moved to the Hermitage only in 1859.

Vessel with a Depiction of Scythians.
Second half of the 4th century B.C.
Kul-Oba kurgan near Kerch, Ukraine.
Gold. 5 ⅛ in. (13 cm) high.
The discovery on September 19, 1831, in
the Kul-Oba kurgan of untouched burials
rich with grave goods is considered the
start of the archaeological study of
antiquity in Russia. The spherical body of
this small gold vessel is decorated with a
relief frieze showing three pairs of men in
Scythian clothing and one stringing a bow.
It may depict the legendary competition
between sons of Heracles, described by
Herodotus: the youngest, Scythes,
managed to string their father's bow and
became the ancestor of the Scythian kings.

RIGHT, TOP

*Belt Plate Showing a Tree, Horses, and
Two Personages over the Body of a Hero.*
5th–4th century B.C. Gold. 4 ¾ in.
(12.1 cm) high, 6 in. (15.2 cm) wide.
This openwork cast and chased plate (like
its symmetrical mirror-image companion)
takes the form of a relief that apparently
depicts a scene from a heroic epic of the
ancient Altai nomads: the revival of a
hero by his wife and brother beneath a
poplar tree. The figures' dress, the
weapons, and the horses' harness look
identical to authentic objects found by
Soviet archaeologists who excavated the
frozen Pazyryk and Tuektin burial
mounds, in the Altai Mountains.

RIGHT, BOTTOM

*Figured Plate in the Form of a Gryphon
Attacking a Horse.* 4th–3rd century B.C.
Gold. 7 ⅝ in. (19.3 cm) long.
The relief on this open-work plate, also
from Peter the Great's Siberian
collection, depicts a horse being attacked
by a horned, lion-headed gryphon, a
subject typical of the Scythians' Animal
Style that evidently related to their
religious conceptions. The vivid
dynamism of the figures of the predatory
monster and its struggling prey combines
with fanciful stylization: the bodies
twisted into an S shape and the
ornamental treatment of the details.
The shoulders, haunches, and eyes of
the animals have sockets for colored
insets now lost.

ABOVE

Headdress in the Form of a Kalathos *Bearing a Depiction of a Battle between the Arimapsi and Gryphons.*
Big Twin burial mound, Bosporan Kingdom, Taman peninsula, Russia. 330–300 B.C. Gold.
4 in. (10 cm) high, 10 ¼ in. (26 cm) diameter.

This ritual headdress in the form of a flared basket, or *kalathos,* is among the priestly attributes associated with the cults of several fertility deities, including Demeter. This richly decorated example consists of thirty interconnected plates. The figurative scene shows a battle between men in barbarian (oriental) clothing and fantastic monsters, one of a group of myths that probably formed in the northern Black Sea area as a result of a symbiosis between the beliefs of the ancient Greek colonists and local legends.

BELOW

Scabbard Cover. Chertomlyk, Dnieper river basin, Ukraine. Third quarter of the 4th century B.C. Gold. 21 ½ in. (54.5 cm) long, 6 ½ in. (16.5 cm), greatest width.

The shape of this scabbard, with a characteristic lobe used to hang it from a belt, is typically Scythian, but the cover was made by a Greek craftsman. Evidently, such articles were specially made in Greek workshops for members of the Scythian elite. Executed in the Greek Classical manner, the battle scene shows Greeks fighting with barbarians and may be an episode from the Trojan War. The scene on the lobe, of a deer being torn apart by a gryphon, is typical of Scythian art.

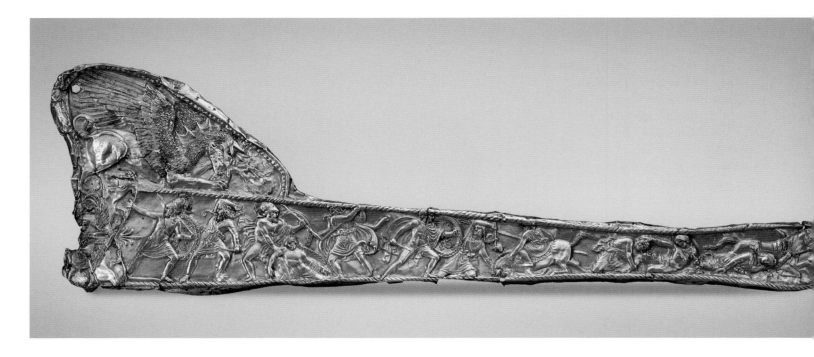

*Temporal Pendant with a Depiction of
a Nereid on a Hippocampus in a
Medallion.* 330–300 B.C. Big Twin burial
mound, Bosporan Kingdom, Taman
peninsula, Russia. Gold and enamel.
6 ⅛ in. (15.5 cm) high.

These pendants (one of the pair is shown)
were attached to each side of the *kalathos*
to dangle at the wearer's temples. The
relief ornament on the medallion shows a
sea nymph, or nereid, riding a
hippocampus, a fantastic mix of horse
and fish. This may be Thetis, the mother
of the ancient Greek hero Achilles, or
one of her companions. The subject
derives from an episode in the *Iliad* in
which Achilles is brought armor made by
Hephaestus, the god of metalworking.

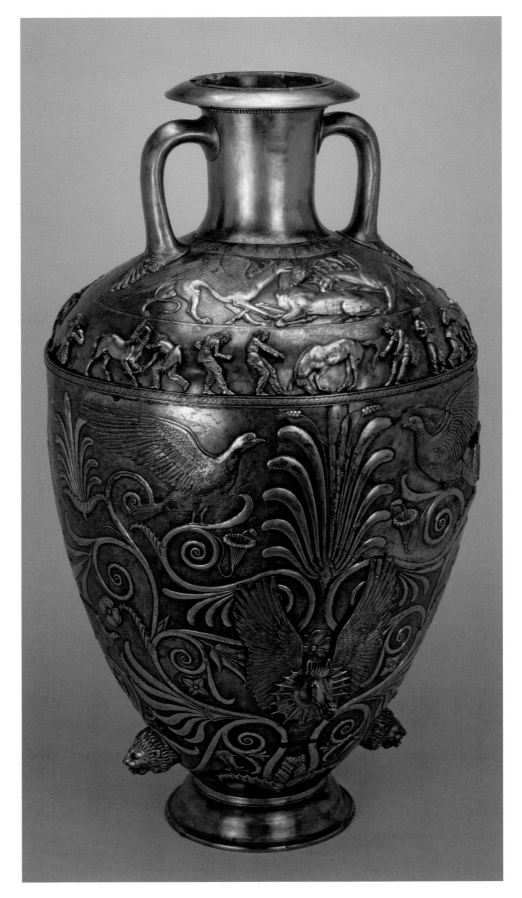

LEFT
Amphora with a Depiction of Scythians.
4th century B.C. Chertomlyk kurgan near
Nikopol, Ukraine. Gilded silver.
27 ½ in. (70 cm) high.
This unique Greek-made amphora was
found in 1863 during excavation of one
of the most famous kurgans in the
Scythian steppes. It is decorated with
gilded relief arranged in tiers. At the top
is a scene of a deer being torn apart by
gryphons; in the middle, Scythians
hobbling horses; below, birds and plant
ornament. Its purpose and symbolism
remain vexed questions, but it was
clearly made by a Greek craftsman
knowledgeable about the Scythians
and their way of life.

OPPOSITE
Male Mask. From a 3rd-century burial
in the Necropolis of Panticapeum; Kerch,
Ukraine. Gold. 10 in. (25.5 cm) high.
A silver dish from the same burial in
which this mask was found bears an
inscription including the name of King
Rescuporides. On this basis, the grave
was determined to be royal and the mask
considered a funerary depiction of the
monarch. But no consensus has been
reached on his identity—eight rulers
of the Bosporan kingdom were named
Rescuporides—or even whether the grave
contains a man or a woman. The plot
thickens with the dating of the mask,
which appears to be older than any other
object in the complex and not originally
intended for a funerary purpose.

Greek and Roman Antiquities

Figured Lekythos in the Form of a Sphinx. Attica. Late 5th–first quarter of the 4th century B.C.
Earthenware. 8 ¼ in. (21 cm) high.

This sphinx-shaped lekythos—a vessel used to store aromatic oils—was discovered in 1869 during the excavation of a female burial in the necropolis of the ancient city of Phanagoria. It is a rare example of the combination of red-figure decoration with polychrome painting applied after firing. The original paints have survived with minimal losses, providing us with an idea of the range of colors used to embellish classical sculpture.

LEFT

Amphora. Third quarter of the 6th century B.C. Earthenware. 12 ½ in. (32 cm) high. Painted amphorae on stands were festive vessels in which wine was served at banquets. In this example, the silhouette of a deer at a watering hole is inscribed within a spacious frame. The empty background contrasts with most near-contemporary examples, whose surfaces are usually covered with painted imagery or patterns.

RIGHT

Red-Figure Pelike. Ca. 510 B.C. Earthenware. 14 ¾ in. (37.5 cm) high. This early red-figure banqueting vessel presents a genre scene: two men in himations on folding *diphros* stools and a naked boy watch the arrival of a swallow. The captions relate the exchange: "Look, a swallow!" / "You're right, by Heracles!" / "Spring has come!" On the other side is a wrestling scene and dedicatory inscription: "The youth Leagros is handsome."

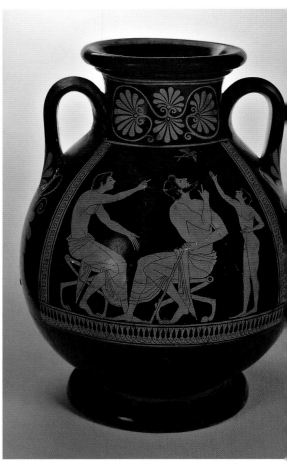

LEFT
Euphonius. *Red-Figure Psykter,
Hetaerae Feasting*. Attica.
505–500 B.C. Earthenware.
14 in. (35.5 cm) high.
   The *psykter*, a rare vessel type,
was filled with ice or cold
water and inserted into a crater
to cool wine at feasts. The four
reclining *hetaerae* (courtesans)
on this example play a drinking
game called *kottaboi*. The object was
to flick the last drops of wine from one's
cup at a target or into another vessel
dedicated to one's beloved.

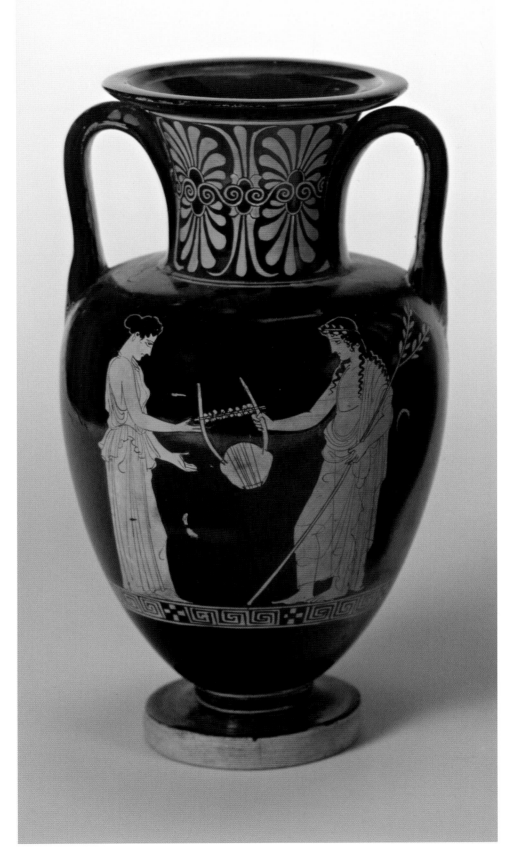

LEFT
Shuvalov painter. *Red-Figure Amphora, Apollo and a Muse*. Attica. Ca. 440 B.C. Earthenware. 9 ½ in. (24 cm) high. This amphora came into the Hermitage in 1928 from the collection of Countess Shuvalova, hence the conventional name of its creator, an unknown vase painter from Attica. More than ten vessels bearing depictions of Apollo and the muses (or other female figures) have been attributed to him. This small, exquisite vessel dates from the political and cultural peak of democratic Athens, a period that also saw the construction of the Acropolis. It shows Apollo Musagetes ("leader of the muses") presenting one of the fabled goddesses with a seven-stringed lyre.

Black-Figure Plate, Dancing Girl. Attica. 500–490 B.C. Painted earthenware. 9 in. (22.9 cm) in diameter.
The dancer wears her hair short and tied with a ribbon, indicating that she is not a freewoman. Her dance with *crotales* (a Greek instrument similar to finger cymbals or castanets) is perhaps for diners at a *symposium*, a convivial gathering often accompanied by performances of dancing girls and female flautists.

Relief, The Death of Niobe's Children.
2nd–1st century B.C. Marble.
18 ⅞ x 76 ⅜ in. (48 x 194 cm).
The story of Niobe was popular with
Greek and Roman artists and poets. The
wife of legendary King Amphion of
Thebes and mother of fourteen children,
Niobe boasted her superiority over the
goddess Leto. In revenge, Leto ordered
her own children, twins Artemis and
Apollo, to massacre her rival's offspring.
A heartbroken Niobe fled and was later
turned to stone.

Statue of Athena. 1st century.
Marble. 65 ¾ in. (167 cm) high.
Athena wears a *chiton*, with sleeves
fastened by three buttons, and a high-
waisted *peplos*. Although this sculpture
dates from Roman times, the pose,
exquisite proportions, and rhythmic
pattern of the clothing's folds indicate
that it may be a copy of a 5th-century-B.C.
work by Kresilas, a pupil of Myron.

Dexamenos of Chios. *Heron Intaglio*.
430s–420s B.C. Chalcedony.
⅞ x ⅝ in. (2.2 × 1.7 cm).
Dexamenos of Chios is the only ancient
Greek gem cutter whose signature is
found on four works. This intaglio
depicting a soaring heron was excavated
in 1860 from an ancient burial near
Kerch. The design was cut with a
diamond point in the fine, slightly
undulating, long lines distinctive of this
master craftsman. The material—pale
blue chalcedony-sapphirine—serves as a
poetic paraphrase of the element in
which the bird soars freely.

Aphrodite and Eros. Boeotia (Tanagra). First quarter of the 3rd century B.C. Terracotta. 7 ¼ in. (18.5 cm) high.
In contrast to most Tanagra statuettes, which were produced in small series, this example is unique. The complex composition required several molds, with the parts attached with slip before firing. Unlike most cult statues of Aphrodite, the goddess is shown seated on a klismos chair with her son in her lap. The rattle was added by a 19th-century restorer. If it were not for the little wings on Eros's back, it would be hard to recognize the Olympian deities in this idyllic composition.

Cameo, "Leda, the Swan, and Eros." Alexandria. 1st century B.C. Sardonyx. ⅞ x 1 ⅛ in. (2.1 x 2.8 cm).
This cameo is attributed to Sostrates, a contemporary of Egypt's queen Cleopatra VII. The erotic scene relates the Greek myth of Zeus assuming the form of a swan to couple with Leda, the wife of King Tyndareus of Sparta. The union produced twins Castor and Pollux and Clytemnestra and Helen, later known as Helen of Troy.

The Taurida Venus. Roman replica of a Hellenistic statue(?). Marble. 66 ½ in. (169 cm) high.
This statue was one of the first ancient sculptures to enter the Hermitage. Acquired in 1721, during the reign of Peter the Great, it adorned the Summer Garden before being moved to the Taurida Palace, for which it is named. The statue is considered to be a Roman copy of a Hellenistic original, but recently it was suggested that it is an authentic Greek cult statue of the 2nd century B.C.

Cameo, Ptolemy II and Arsinoe II (Gonzaga Cameo). Alexandria. 3rd century B.C. Agate. 6 ⅛ x 4 ⅝ in. (15.7 x 11.8 cm).
This masterpiece of official art depicts Ptolemy II Philadelphus ("sister-loving") and Arsinoe II Philadelpha ("brother-loving"), rulers of Hellenistic Egypt, as Olympian gods. The queen's head shawl symbolizes the new deities' sacred marriage. Marriage between close relatives and deification of living monarchs were customary in ancient Egypt, and so were also used to establish the continuity and legitimacy of nonnative dynasties.

Greek and Roman Antiquities   93

ABOVE

Portrait of Livia. 1st century A.D. Marble. 13 ⅜ in. (34 cm) high.

Livia Drusilla (58 B.C.–A.D. 29) was the first Roman woman in whose honor altars were constructed and statues erected. At age 20, she married the emperor Augustus and, after his death, enjoyed nearly unlimited power. The portrait head (part of a larger statue) presents her in the guise of Ceres-Augusta, high priestess of the cult of Divine Augustus.

Statue of Augustus in the Guise of Jupiter.
First half of the 1st century. Marble.
72 ⅞ in. (185 cm) high.
The Italian neoclassical sculptor Filippo
Gnaccarini, who restored this badly
damaged statue found during excavations
at Cumae, added to it the attributes of
Jupiter (a scepter and figure of Victory on
an orb). Augustus was indeed depicted in
this way in the reigns of his successors,
beginning with Tiberius (r. A.D. 14–37),
who established the official cult of the
deified late emperor.

OPPOSITE

Colossal Statue of Jupiter. Late 1st century A.D. Marble, bronzed plaster. 136 ⅝ in. (347 cm) high.

Despite its impressive size, this work is only one-third as tall as its legendary prototype by Phidias at Olympia, one of the Seven Wonders of the ancient world. Although he took the general composition from Phidias's famous work, the unknown Roman sculptor used different materials: marble and gilded wood instead of sheets of ivory and gold. The statue was found in pieces and restored, with the lost wooden elements (the *himation*, eagle, and attributes of the god) remade in gilded plaster.

RIGHT

Female Portrait, "The Syrian Woman." Ca. A.D. 160. Marble. 11 ⅞ in. (30 cm) high.

This splendid portrait of unknown origin belonged to a statue depicting a member of the Roman elite. The elaborate coiffure reflects the fashion popular in the time of the mid-2nd-century Antonine emperors. Like the emperors themselves, the woman may have been North African. Her Semitic features have prompted the work's conventional title: "The Syrian Woman."

Sarcophagus, Hippolytus and Phaedra.
Attica. Mid-3rd century. Marble.
49 ¼ in. (125 cm) high.
According to Greek myth, the passionate
hunter Hippolytus angered Aphrodite by
his preference for Artemis. Aphrodite
exacted revenge by making Phaedra, his
father's young wife, fall in love with him.
The sarcophagus shows the moment
when Hippolytus rejects Phaedra's
advances, setting off a chain of tragic
events that ended in Phaedra's suicide
and Hippolytus's death.

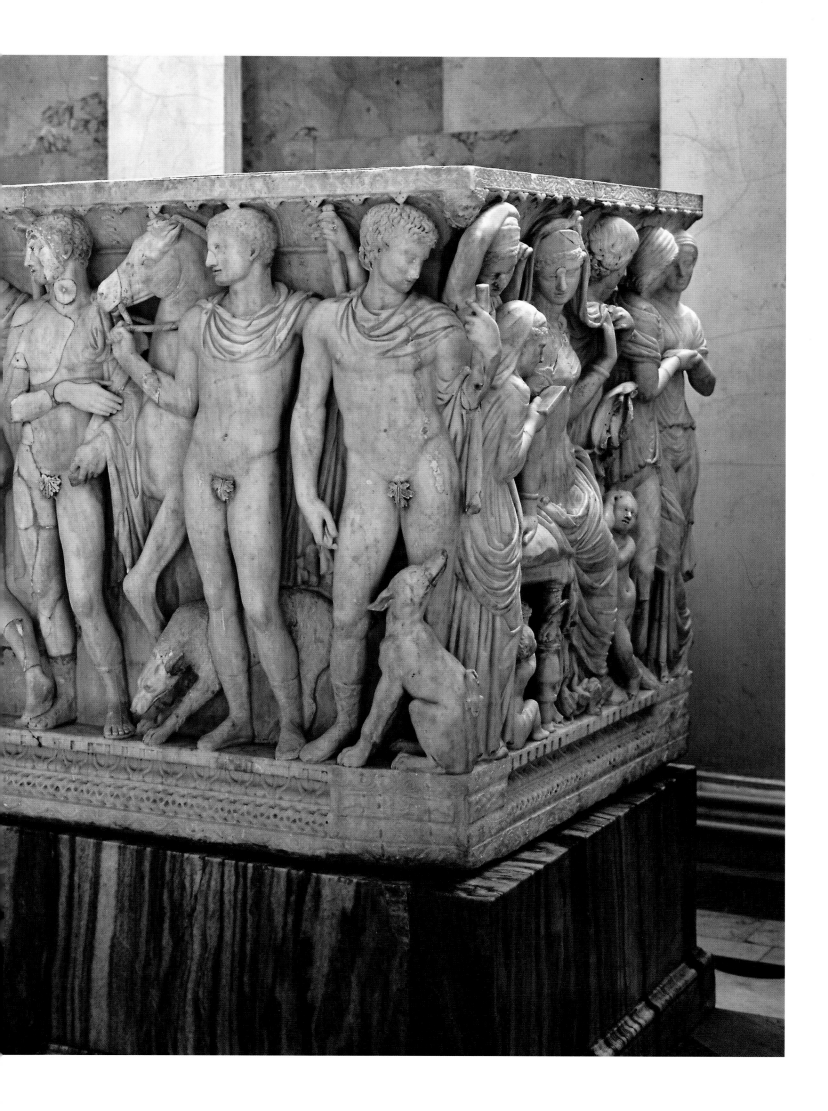

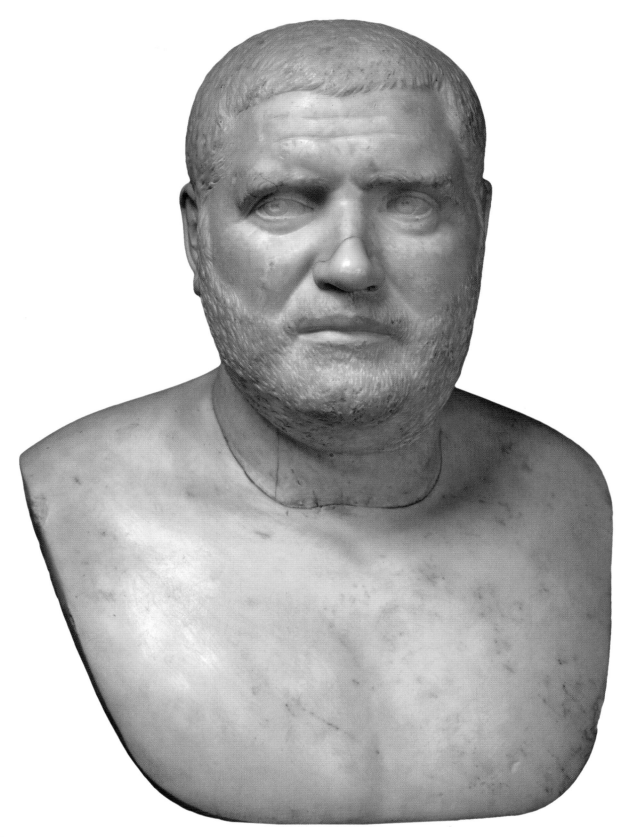

Portrait of Emperor Philip the Arab. Second half of the 3rd century. Marble. 27 ½ in. (70 cm) high.
Marcus Julius Philippus (ca. 200–249), known as Philip the Arab, rose to the high military position of prefect of the Pretorian Guard and in 244 crowned himself emperor. According to the *Augustan Histories*, he was "a man of low birth, but haughty" who gained power "by dishonest means," by killing his co-ruler. He ruled only five years before dying in a battle for the throne.

Portrait of Emperor Balbinus. Second quarter of the 3rd century. Marble. 28 ½ in. (72.5 cm) high.
The features of this aged emperor made wise by the years bear the stamp of sorrow. This characterization in the posthumous portrait is supported by facts: Balbinus was proclaimed emperor jointly with Pupienus Maximus at a time of civil strife. He reportedly died during a mutiny just ninety-nine days later.

Byzantine and Ancient Russian Art

Christ Pantocrator. Northern Painting. Second half of the 13th century. Egg tempera on panel with a fine layer of gesso. 25 ⅜ x 16 ⅜ in. (64.5 × 41.5 cm).

This icon is among the four earliest works in the Hermitage belonging to the circle known as Northern Painting—the ecclesiastical art of the remoter regions of Novgorodian territory. Christ is depicted on a black background, giving the blessing with his right hand and holding an open Gospel in his left. Stylistic and iconographic features that include a certain simplification of the image and attention to the ornamentation of the clothing indicate that the icon was created in one of the centers of northern European Russia.

ABOVE

Bottom of a Vessel with a Depiction of the Sacrifice of Isaac. Rome. 4th century. Two-layer glass, gold. 3 ¾ in. (9.5 cm). The Old Testament scene was engraved on extremely fine gold foil sandwiched between layers of clear glass. Although the unevenness of the edge of this object gives it the look of being a fragment, such pieces may have been specially made in this way for ritual use—probably for inclusion in early Christian burials. The Hermitage exhibit and several analogous items were found in the Roman catacombs.

A Silenus and a Maenad. Dish. Constantinople. 610–29. Silver with gilding. 10 ⅛ in. (25.7 cm) diameter.
Depicted here are a silenus dancing with a wineskin over his shoulders and a maenad accompanying the dance with
percussion instruments like a cymbal or crotales. The group is compositionally inscribed into a circle. The figures have
been left ungilded and stand out in relief from the cut-away gilded background. The dish has been dated by five marks
from the reign of Emperor Heraclius (610–641) punched into the reverse.

OPPOSITE

Diptych with Church Scenes.
Constantinople (?)/Alexandria (?).
5th century. Carved ivory. Each panel
13 x 4 ⅛ in. (33 x 10.5 cm).
In contrast to the majority of early
Byzantine ivory diptychs, this example
does not depict a consul embarking on
the office to which there were annual
elections in Constantinople. It probably
served as an invitation to the games held
in the capital's hippodrome each year
on January 1, on the occasion of the
consular elections.

RIGHT

Leaf of a Diptych of Consul Areobindus.
Constantinople. 506. Carved ivory.
14 ⅞ x 5 ½ in. (37.6 x 14 cm).
Consul Areobindus sits in an armchair at
the opening of the circus games and
signals for the spectacle to begin. Flavius
Areobindus Dagalaiphus, "a man of
nobility" as the inscription above
proclaims, was a Goth by origin who
married a granddaughter of Emperor
Valentinian III (r. 425–55). He held the
office of consul in the Byzantine capital
in 506, under Emperor Anastasius I
(r. 491–518). The sceptre in his left hand
ends in a depiction of the emperor
presenting the consul with a scroll that
lists his rights.

The Forty Martyrs of Sebaste. Triptych. Turn of the 11th century. Elephant ivory; silver mount and coloring are of later date. 7 ¼ x 9 ⅝ in. (18.5 × 24.3 cm) (open).

This triptych is a masterpiece from Byzantium's Macedonian Renaissance. The central scene depicts a legend of the time when Emperor Constantine ruled jointly with Licinius (around 320). On their commander's orders, 40 Christian converts from the garrison of Sebaste, in Asia Minor, were driven naked onto a frozen lake and left there for the night. The icon shows one man unable to bear the agony, taking refuge in a building on the shore, but his place is immediately taken by one of the guards. Like many Byzantine ivories, this triptych was tinted. Apart from the easily identifiable blue background and gilding, light blue, green, and pink dyes were also used.

Saints George and Demetrius of Thessalonika. Late 11th–early 12th century. Carved dark slate with gilding. 7 ⅞ x 5 ½ in. (19.9 × 14 cm).

This icon depicting the holy warriors George and Demetrius was found in 1894 at Chersonesus, in the Crimea, during excavations of a building believed to be a warehouse. It was shattered into at least 15 fragments, some of which were not found, although eight men sifted the soil of its location for two days. Iconographic and stylistic peculiarities identify it as coming from a Thessalonian workshop. The closest analogy for the figure of Demetrius is found on the bottom of a Byzantine serpentine bowl now in the treasury of St. Mark's in Venice.

The Transfiguration. Byzantium. 12th century. Egg tempera on panel. 9 ⅛ x 9 ⅜ in. (23.2 × 23.7 cm).

This icon was part of the *epithelium*, a horizontal board depicting the great Christian feasts that came above the local tier in an iconostasis. Traces of the fastening can be seen on the reverse. The Byzantine Museum in Athens and the Vatopedi Monastery on Mount Athos have two more fragments of the same epithelium, which was evidently sawn up. The archaeologist Piotr Sevastyanov brought this icon to Russia from Mount Athos in 1860. Although the red ground is not typical for Byzantine icons, it is not unknown in the medieval period. Red had great symbolic meaning in Byzantine iconography: it represented not only fire and purification but also the blood of Christ.

ABOVE

The Holy Warriors George, Theodore, and Demetrius. Constantinople. Late 11th–early 12th century. Tempera on chestnut panel. 11 ¼ x 14 ⅛ in. (28.5 × 36 cm).

Saints George, Theodore, and Demetrius were supposed to have appeared to help the Crusaders during the siege of Antioch in 1098. Small portable icons of these warrior saints were particularly popular with the military aristocracy, who took them on campaigns and prayed in front of them before battles. The intricate miniature method of painting, with techniques that combine visualization of the mystic understanding of the world that emerged in Byzantine theology in the 11th century and quaintly interpreted Hellenistic traditions, indicates that the icon was created by a Constantinopolitan artist.

P. 112

St. Gregory Thaumaturge. Constantinople. First half of the 12th century. Tempera on walnut panel.
31 ⅞ x 20 ⅞ in. (81 × 53 cm).

This icon depicts Gregory, the sainted Bishop of Neocaesarea (ca. 213–270/275). An outstanding missionary and theologian, Gregory was a pupil of Origen of Alexandria, one of the foremost Fathers of the Church, and himself among those who formulated the doctrine of the Trinity. The Hermitage work is a masterpiece of Byzantine icon-painting. The artist produced an individualized, almost portrait image. Proper appreciation of the work is somewhat marred by the loss of the precious metal mount that originally covered the icon, as is evidenced by the well-preserved margins and the marks of fastenings.

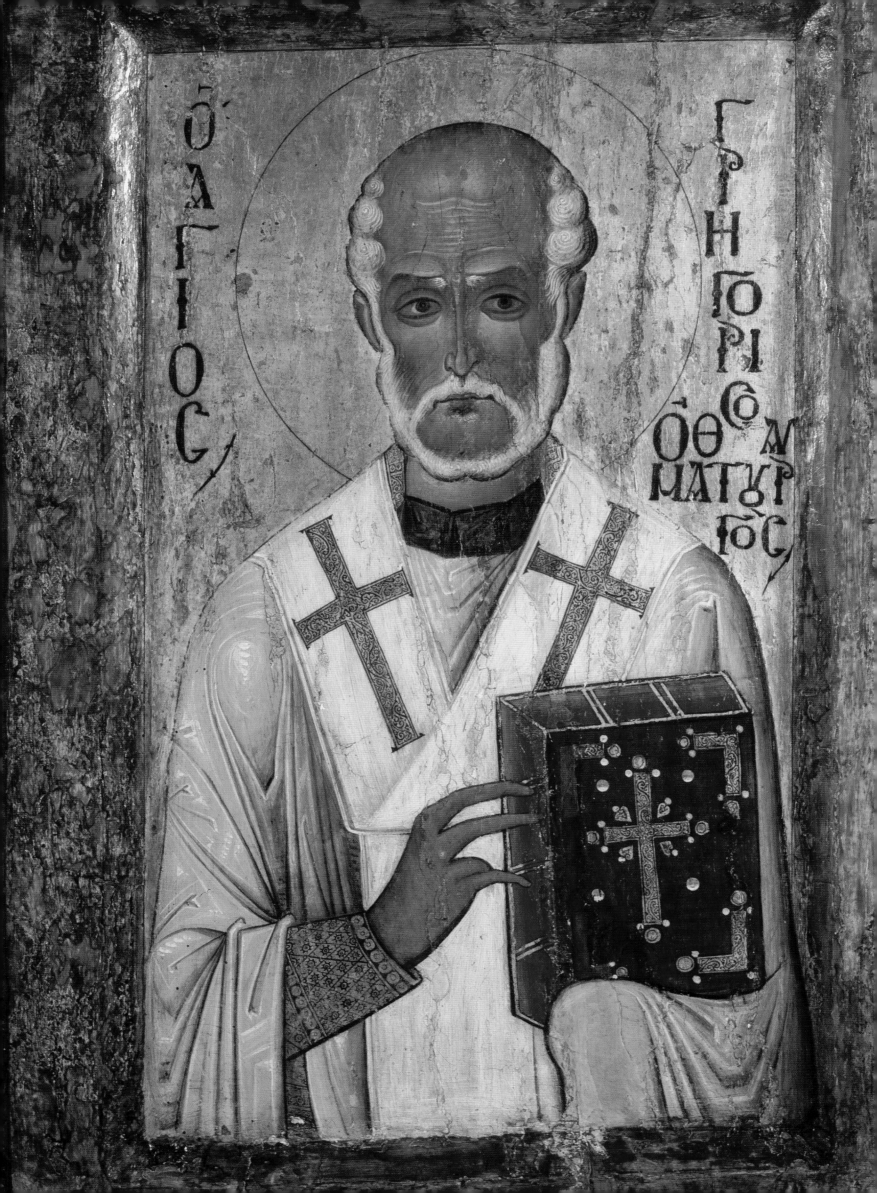

Ο ΑΓΙΟC ΓΡΗΓΟΡΙΟC Ο ΘΑΥΜΑΤΥΡΓΟC

Christ Pantocrator. 1363. Egg tempera on panel. 41 ¾ x 31 ⅛ in. (106 x 79 cm).

The donors depicted in the margin of the icon were members of the imperial family who founded the Church of the Pantocrator on Mount Athos in 1363, also the date of the icon's creation. Christ is shown holding a Gospel in his left hand while the right is raised in a gesture of blessing.

The Epiphany. Pskov. Mid-14th century. Egg tempera on gessoed panel. 35 ⅞ x 26 ½ in. (90 × 67.5 cm). One of the few Pskovian icons in the Hermitage collection is notable for the unusual manner of painting, reminiscent of fresco technique, and treatment of the subject: the baptism of Christ by John the Baptist. Such unusual details as the absence of a scroll associated with John and Christ's naked body derive from early sources. Untypical also for the iconography of Christ's baptism is the lack of a symbolic depiction of the Holy Spirit.

St. Nicholas the Wonder-Worker. Novgorod. Late 13th–early 14th century. Egg tempera on gessoed panel. 42 ⅜ x 31 ¼ in. (107.7 × 79.5 cm). Nicholas, the most highly venerated saint in Early Rus', is depicted half-length in this Novgorodian icon, giving a blessing with his right hand and holding the Gospel in his left, which is covered by the end of his omophorion (a liturgical stole worn by Orthodox bishops). This iconography of the saint is traditional for 13th-century Novgorod. The red background is a characteristic feature of the Novgorodian school of icon-painting.

P. 116

The Intercession of the Virgin. 15th century. Egg tempera on gessoed panel. 29 ⅛ x 20 x 1 in. (74 × 51 × 2.5 cm). The intercession of the Virgin on behalf of humankind is symbolized by a veil that she spread over worshippers in a vision that took place in a Constantinople church in 910, when Byzantium was under threat from the Saracens. The vision was witnessed by the holy fool Andrew. He and his young companion Epiphanius are among the saints depicted in the icon. The Feast of the Intercession, established by the Eastern Church in memory of this event, is particularly celebrated in Russia.

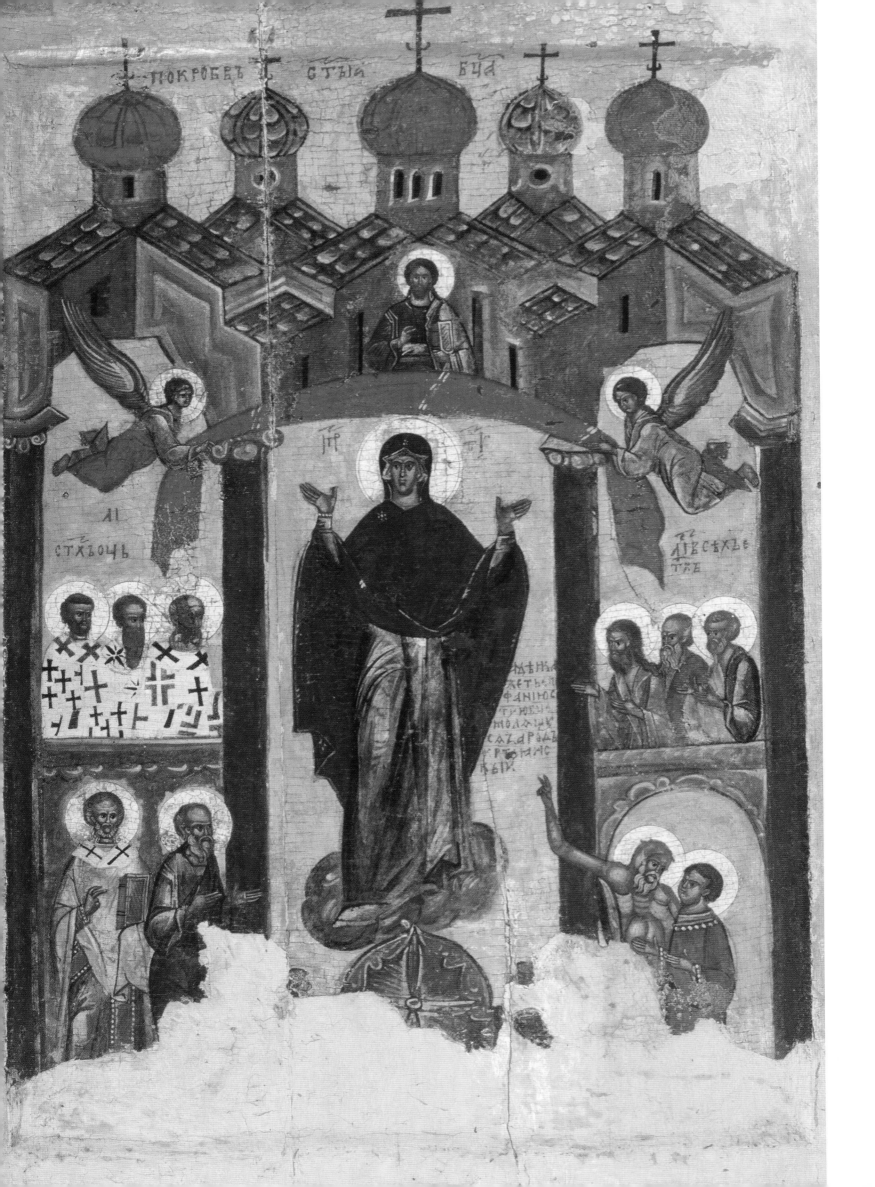

RIGHT

St. Nicholas, with Scenes from His Life (Nicholas of Zaraisk). Novgorod. First half of the 16th century. Egg tempera on gessoed panel with gilding. 65 x 45 ¼ in. (165 × 115 cm).

One traditional Russian type of icon depicted a saint in the center surrounded by marginal scenes of his life. In this case, these include the birth of St. Nicholas, his consecration as deacon and bishop, and his miracles. Some subjects do not appear in other icons. The saint is shown in his bishop's robes, his right hand raised in blessing, his left holding the Gospel. Legend has it that the Byzantine prototype for this version was brought to the town of Zaraisk in the 13th century.

P. 118

The Last Judgement. Novgorod. 16th century. Egg tempera on gessoed panel with gilding. 69 ⅜ x 47 ¼ in. (177 × 120 cm).

This elaborate, multifigure composition has, at the top, Christ in judgment surrounded by the apostles. The angels rolling up the sky symbolize the end of the world. Below, on the left, is an allegorical depiction of Paradise; on the right are the Earth and Sea, represented by two female figures almost in the spirit of classical antiquity, giving up their dead. The complex symbolism is the product of many written sources: the Gospels and Apocalypse, and works by Byzantine and early Russian authors.

The Transfiguration. Novgorod. 16th century. Egg tempera on gessoed panel with gilding. 30 ¾ x 24 in. (78 × 61 cm). The Gospel account of Christ in Glory on the summit of Mount Tabor is presented here in brief and with certain peculiarities. Christ's right hand, for example, is open and not closed in a gesture of blessing. The whiteness of his clothing is stressed by the dark background in the form of a red six-pointed star with gold rays, inscribed in a circle instead of the traditional almond-shaped mandorla.

Medieval European Decorative Arts

Circle of Colin Noualier. *The Mocking of Christ*. Limoges. Second quarter of the 16th century. Copper, enamel, polychrome painting, and clear counter-enamelling. 8 ⅛ x 6 ⅜ in. (20.6 x 16.3 cm).

Painted enamel plaques assembled into miniature altarpieces were popular in the 16th century. The series of 12 plaques depicting the Passion to which this example belongs was based on engravings by Lucas van Leyden. Graphic prototypes were typical for the "new school" of Limoges enamel that emerged in the 1530s.

ABOVE

Reliquary of St. Valerie. Limoges. Ca. 1175. Wood, engraved copper with champlevé enamel, and gilding. 11 in. (27.7 cm) high.

Among the masterpieces of Romanesque art produced in Limoges workshops is this reliquary casket bearing scenes from the life of Valerie, the daughter of the ruler of Aquitaine and one of the city's patron saints. As an ardent convert to Christianity, Valerie refused to marry the pagan Roman proconsul who sought her hand, so he ordered her to be beheaded. Then a miracle occurred: the dead martyr picked up her own head and carried it to her mentor, Saint Martial.

RIGHT

Reliquary of St. Stephen. France. Late 12th century. Wood, silver, and precious and semiprecious stones. 16 ¾ in. (42.5 cm) high.

One of the first Christian priests, Saint Stephen suffered a martyr's death by stoning for preaching the new faith. This statuette served as a container for a sacred relic, now lost, that originally fit into an irregularly shaped socket inside the book the saint is holding.

P. 124, LEFT

Processional Cross. Limoges. First quarter of the 13th century. Wood, copper, brass, opaque enamel (champlevé technique), glass, gilding. 23 x 14 ½ in. (58.7 × 37 cm).

On feast days associated with the Holy Cross, crosses like this were carried on poles in procession or placed on a special stand on the altar. Some particularly valuable examples contained particles of the "True Cross," discovered in Jerusalem around the year 320. This example has a wooden core covered with brass sheets and is decorated with enamel insets and applied figures of the crucified Christ, Mary, and St. John. The back features Christ in a mandorla, with the symbols of the Evangelists at the ends of the arms.

OPPOSITE
Pyx Depicting the Virgin and Child.
Limoges. Mid-13th century. Opaque
enamel on copper (champlevé
technique) with glass.
15 ½ in. (39 cm) high.
This reliquary takes the form of the
Virgin Mary and the Christ Child seated
on a cubic throne; the pierced balustrade
is identical to the characteristic
decoration on the crests of Limoges
caskets. The throne's side walls show an
Annunciation scene, while at the back is
a little door that, researchers suggest,
indicates this sculptural group was used
to store the consecrated Host.

RIGHT
Plaque with a Depiction of a Saint.
Western Europe (?). 19th century (?).
Opaque enamel on copper with gilding.
2 ¾ x 1 ½ in. (7 × 4.2 cm).
This plaque bearing a three-quarter-
length depiction of an unknown saint
came into the Hermitage in 1924.
Stylistically it is close to a group of early
enamels from the workshop of Abbot
Begon, who worked at the Sainte-Foy
monastery in Conques in the early 12th
century. But several features—the color
of the enamels and the use of the
champlevé (rather than a combination
with cloisonné)—cast doubt on its
authenticity. Technical studies have
borne this out, and it is probably a skillful
19th-century stylization.

Reliquary of St. Elizabeth of Hungary.
France. Mid-13th century. Wood, silver,
precious and semiprecious stones, glass.
22 ⅞ in. (58 cm) high.

This reliquary in the form of an
architectural pediment framing a figure
of Saint Elizabeth was made by Parisian
jewelers. Elizabeth's name is given in an
inscription on the base. The daughter
of a Hungarian king, Elizabeth was
married at an early age to a duke of
Thuringia, who soon died on his way
to the Crusades. The widowed duchess
devoted herself to caring for the sick and
impoverished, becoming a symbol
of Christian charity. She was canonized
within five years of her death.

Triptych with a Depiction of the Virgin and Child with Angels. Northern France (?). First third of the 14th century. Carved ivory and wood. 13 x 11 ¼ in. (32.8 × 28.5 cm).

French, and particularly Parisian, ivory-carving had its heyday in the 13th and 14th centuries. Aristocrats and wealthy burghers commissioned diptychs and triptychs decorated with ivory reliefs whose complex compositions featured superbly executed miniature figures and architectural decor. In surviving property inventories, such items figured among those taken on journeys. Scenes from the life of the Virgin were favorite subjects; medieval hymns compared Mary to an ivory tower as the embodiment of purity.

LEFT

The Virgin and Child. France. First half of the 14th century. Ivory with traces of paint, metal, precious stones, filigree work. 17 ¾ in. (45 cm) high.

Figures like this, reproducing a type that had formed in large-scale Gothic statuary, were intended for the domestic chapels of wealthy families. In them Mary has lost the static, stern expressiveness of Romanesque works and acquired features of a courtly lady. The natural curve of her figure is emphasized by the folds of the cloak, which the craftsman delineated with great skill.

BELOW

Panel of a Diptych with a Depiction of the Crucifixion. Germany. Late 14th century. Carved ivory, with traces of green paint. 6 x 3 ⅜ in. (15 x 8.5 cm).

Such diptychs, reproducing in miniature the large altar compositions that adorned medieval cathedrals, served as an aid to prayer in domestic chapels or on journeys. When depicting Gospel events, irrespective of where they occurred, Gothic ivory-carvers always placed them in an architectural setting. Besides providing compositional completeness and decorative effect, this approach enabled them to give their miniature devotional pieces greater similarity to church interiors.

ABOVE

Agraffe with a Depiction of the Virgin and Saints. 15th century. Lower Saxony. Copper and silver with gilding. 8 ½ in. (21.5 cm) high.

Once kept in Cologne Cathedral, this massive clasp for a bishop's vestments was acquired by Alexander Bazilevsky in 1874 and came into the Hermitage as part of his collection. It bears relief images of the Virgin and Saints Helen, Andrew, and James with little figures of angels making music. It is an early example of a signed medieval work. A German inscription reads: "I, Derick the jeweler, undertook to make the clasp entirely from copper apart from the four silver depictions." Latin inscriptions on banderoles give the names of the nine orders of angels.

Workshop of the Master of the Orleans. *Triptych: Carrying the Cross; Crucifixion; Lamentation*. France. Late 15th–early 16th century. Copper, enamel, wood, silver mounts, with polychrome painting and gilding. 11 ⅞ x 15 in. (30 x 38 cm). The abundant use of enamel cabochons—drop-shaped convex projections with foil beneath—was characteristic of "old school" Limoges enamelers, including this workshop. Another distinctive feature is the virtuoso way the clothing folds have been painted in gold. The central Crucifixion scene features angels collecting blood flowing from Christ's hands. The soul of Dismas, the penitent thief to Christ's right, is shown as an infant being carried away by an angel, while the unrepentant Gestas's soul is taken by a devil.

ABOVE

Workshop of the Pénicauds (?). *Casket with Scenes from the Life of St. Margaret.* Limoges. First
third of the 16th century. Copper, enamel, bronze, wood, polychrome painting, gilding, and clear counter-enameling.
6 ⅞ x 3 ¾ x 4 ⅜ in. (17.5 x 9.5 x 11.3 cm).

The casket is embellished with 12 enameled plaques, 10 of which bear a *P* beneath a crown, a mark associated with
the Pénicaud dynasty of Limoges. The plaques depict episodes from the life of St. Margaret of Antioch, an early
Christian martyr venerated in France in the 15th and 16th centuries. One shows a monk holding a severed foot.
A reliquary is known to have been created at Limoges in the 1520s to hold St. Margaret's foot, and this casket may
also have been a reliquary.

ABOVE

The Entombment. Second third of the 16th century. Copper, enamel, polychrome painting, and clear counter-
enameling. 8 ⅛ x 6 ½ in. (20.6 x 16.5 cm).

This plaque's subject derives from the Gospel of St. John (19:39–42). In the foreground Joseph of Arimathea and
Nicodemus are shown lowering Christ's body into a coffin. Stylistic peculiarities of the enamel painting, the color
scheme, and the faces depicted with straight noses and pointed beards make it possible to attribute it to the circle
of craftsmen who worked in the manner of Colin Noualier.

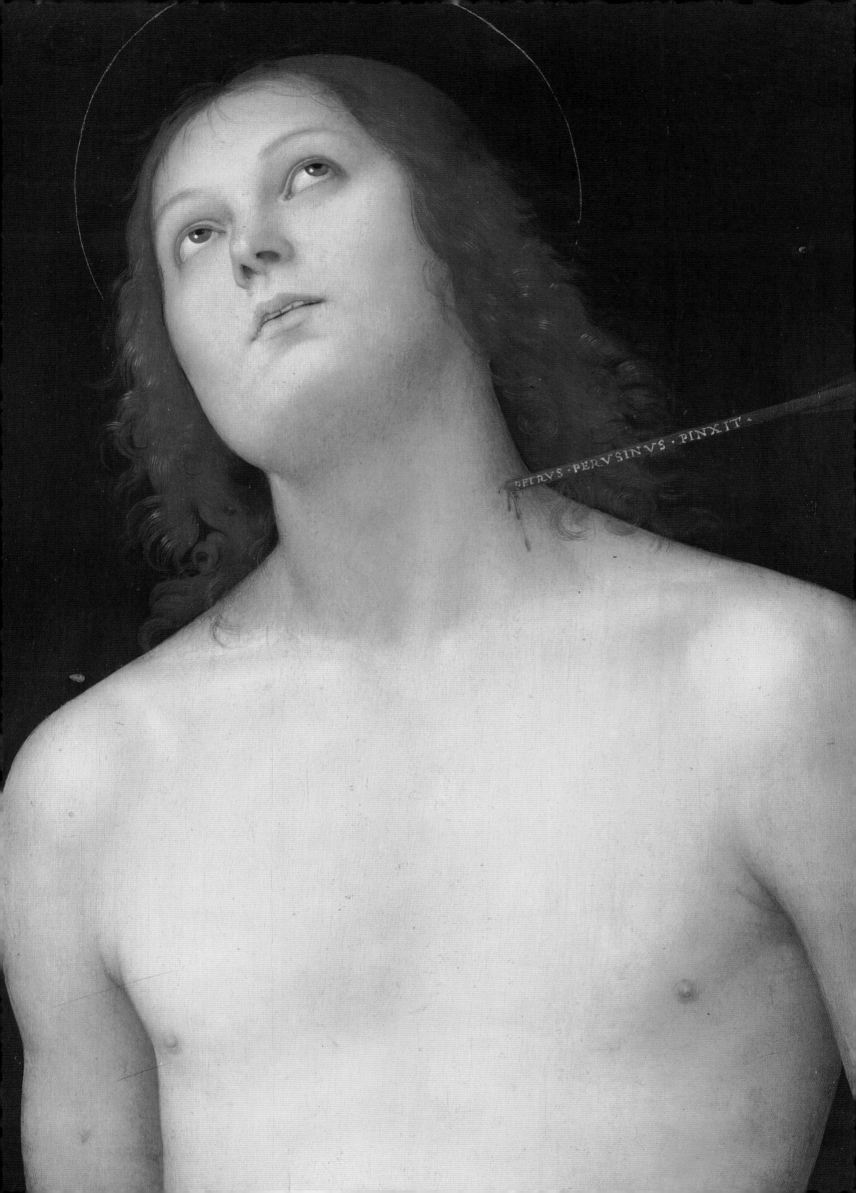

PETRVS · PERVSINVS · PINXIT ·

Western European Painting, 13th–Early 18th Century

OPPOSITE
Pietro Perugino (Pietro Vanucci). *St. Sebastian*. Between 1493 and 1494. Tempera and oil on panel.
21 ⅛ x 15 ½ in. (53.8 x 39.5 cm).

The martyrdom of St. Sebastian was a popular subject in Renaissance panting. According to legend, none of the arrows shot into his body caused a mortal wound; artists most often ignored that detail, however. Perugino depicts the saint with an arrow through the neck and, surprisingly, places his signature on the shaft, the very instrument of martyrdom.

ABOVE

Ugolino di Tedice. *Cross with a Crucifixion*. Ca. 1270. Tempera on panel. 35 ½ x 24 ½ in. (90 x 62 cm).
The trecento was the seedbed for the Renaissance that, in the following two centuries, would make painting a mirror of nature and a means of artistic self-expression. In this Pisan cross, however, nothing yet suggests such changes. Depicting the grieving Mary and St. John in squares at the ends of the arms of the cross, the artist seeks not to present a scene of prayerful intercession but concisely and unequivocally to remind the viewer of the agonies that Christ took upon himself.

OPPOSITE

Antonio di Firenze. *Madonna and Child with a Sainted Bishop, John the Baptist, and Angels*.
First half of the 15th century. Tempera on panel. 59 ½ x 33 ½ in. (151 x 85 cm).
This double-sided work was meant to be carried in religious processions. The name of the saint on the left is written in his halo but partially covered by his bishop's mitre. Because he is shown holding a tower, scholars have suggested it may be Liberius of Ravenna or Zenobius of Florence. The Crucifixion scene on the reverse repeats the composition by Fra Angelico in the church of the Montecarlo monastery, in San Giovanni Valdarno, outside Florence. The depiction at the foot of the Cross—of monks holding scourges and wearing hoods that cover the head, with only slits for the eyes— suggests that this work was commissioned by the Capuchin order.

Ugolino Lorenzetti. *Calvary*. Ca. 1350. Tempera on panel. 36 x 21 ⅞ in. (91.5 x 55.5 cm).
This altarpiece is probably among the early works of a Sienese artist active between 1320 and 1360. It displays features that derive from the Byzantine artistic tradition: the depiction of figures on different scales, the placement of the groups, and architecture shown from several viewpoints simultaneously. Ugolino Lorenzetti's later paintings are closer to Gothic art, demonstrating the artist's familiarity with the work of Simone Martini and Pietro Lorenzetti.

Simone Martini. *The Virgin from an* Annunciation. 1339–42. Tempera on panel. 12 x 8 ½ in. (30.5 x 21.5 cm).
Simone Martini, a pupil of Duccio, brought fame to his native Siena as the foremost artistic center in Italy. His refined, exquisite style impressed aristocratic customers. Petrarch called him "the master of our time," and according to Vasari the epitaph above the artist's tomb in the Sienese monastery of San Domenico read: "To the most celebrated of all painters." Here, Martini's archangel is holding not a lily, a symbol of purity traditional for this subject, but an olive branch. The choice may have stemmed from the lily's association with Siena's rival city, Florence.

Spinello Aretino (Spinello di Luca Spinelli). *Polyptych Panels: Saints Benedict and Pontian*. Between 1383 and 1384. Tempera on panel. 51 ⅛ x 16 ⅜ in. (130 x 41.5 cm). The monastery of San Ponziano in the Italian town of Lucca, where the artist worked between 1380 and 1385, belonged to the Olivetan order, which explains the unusual attire of St. Benedict. Aretino has shown him in the white habit of the Olivetan congregation rather than in black, as is traditional for the Benedictines.

Fra Angelico (Guido di Pietro). *The Virgin and the Child with Saints Dominic and Thomas Aquinas.*
Between 1424 and 1430. Fresco. 77 ⅛ x 73 ⅝ in. (196 x 187 cm).
This work is part of a fresco cycle the artist created in the San Domenico monastery in Fiesole, where he was prior.
Angelico's devotion to his religious calling, in both life and art, did not prevent him from becoming an innovator in
painting. Without pursuing the dynamic action and spatial depth sought by most of his contemporaries, he achieves a
sculpture-like monumentality that—like the airy translucence of his paints, especially those in the murals—links this
artist with the refined intellectual Piero della Francesca.

Fra Filippo Lippi. *The Vision of St. Augustine*. Late 1450s–early 1460s. Tempera and oil on panel.
11 x 20 ¼ in. (28 x 51.5 cm).
The subject here, rare in Italian art, is from the life of St. Augustine of Hippo (354–430). According to legend, one day while pondering the mystery of the Trinity, the bishop had a vision of a child who was using a spoon to transfer water from the sea into a small puddle. In response to Augustine's question, the child explained that his pursuit was no less futile than the bishop's attempts to understand the Trinity. In Fra Filippo Lippi's version, the sea is represented by a stream, and the Trinity takes the form of a disk with a fiery aureole containing three profiles.

LEFT

Filippino Lippi. *Adoration of the Christ Child*. Mid-1480s. Oil on copper. 20 ⅞ in. (53 cm) diameter.

Filippino Lippi, the son of Fra Filippo Lippi, studied painting under Botticelli, one of the most brilliant members of the Medici school formed at Lorenzo the Magnificent's court in Florence. This tondo is typical of the Medici circle. The treatment of the Nativity as the adoration of the Christ Child derives from 14th-century mystic literature. The *Celestial Revelations* of St. Bridget of Sweden states that, when the time came for the Virgin Mary to give birth, she went down on her knees and began to pray: "Suddenly in a moment she gave birth to her son, from whom radiated such an ineffable light and splendor that the sun was not comparable to it, nor did the candle that St. Joseph had put there give any light at all."

Filippino Lippi. *Annunciation*. Between 1490 and 1496. Tempera on panel. 13 ¾ x 19 ⅞ in. (35 x 50.5 cm). Although not in the least concerned about historical authenticity, Filippino Lippi also did not, it seems, strive to convincingly portray contemporary Italian life. The architectural division of the room and its rather illogically placed contents serve to create the illusion of depth by means of foreshortening. In that regard, the painting possesses meticulous clarity and, under the guise of a touching domestic scene, presents a precisely drawn geometrical projection.

Sandro Botticelli (Alessandro di Mariano dei Filipepi). *St. Dominic*. 1490s. Tempera and oil on canvas (transferred from panel). 17 ½ x 10 ¼ in. (44.5 x 26 cm).
Botticelli was a pupil of Fra Filippo Lippi and one of the most gifted painters working at the court of Lorenzo the Magnificent. Here the founder of the Dominican order of monks is presented in an iconographic manner that is rarely found: above the saint, whose hand is raised in a gesture of blessing, is a half-figure of Christ surrounded by angels heralding the Last Judgment. It has been suggested that this painting was a sort of response to Savonarola's execution, in May 1498: Botticelli is said to have been one of his followers.

Pietro Perugino (Pietro Vannucci). *Portrait of a Young Man*. Ca. 1500. Oil on canvas (transferred from panel). 17 ¾ x 10 in. (45 x 25.5 cm).

The "dove-like gaze"—as contemporaries described the dreamily pious visual appeal to heaven that typifies Perugino's personages—is also seen in this secular painting. Identification of the model is complicated by the artist's evident indifference to the depiction of individual characteristics and achievements. But it is the very impersonality that is remarkable in the portraits of an artist who was more concerned with the compositional arrangement of figures and spatial rhythm.

Lorenzo Costa. *Female Portrait*. 1500–1505. Tempera and oil on canvas (transferred from panel). 22 ½ x 17 ⅜ in. (57 x 44 cm).

A prolific artist of the late 15th century, Lorenzo Costa worked in Bologna beginning about 1483. In 1507 he entered the service of the house of Gonzaga in Mantua, where he painted Marchesa Isabella d'Este and the poet Battista Fiera. The subject of this portrait may have been Emilia Pia da Montefeltro (1471–1528), an educated member of the Urbino aristocracy.

ABOVE

Giovanni Battista Cima da Conegliano. *Annunciation*. 1495. Oil on canvas (transferred from panel). 53 ½ x 42 ⅛ in. (136 x 107 cm).

In the illusory space skillfully created by perspective, the divine light that, by medieval tradition, accompanied the Archangel Gabriel as he brought Mary the news of Christ's conception seems real. We do not immediately notice that this source—and not the sun—illuminates the messenger. A rush of air bursts into the room with him, fluttering his robe, hair, and even the paper that carries a list of those who commissioned the work as well as the artist's signature.

Leonardo da Vinci. *Madonna with the Child (Litta Madonna)*. 1490–91. Tempera on canvas (transferred from panel). 16 ½ x 13 in. (42 x 33 cm).

Leonardo is one of those rare geniuses for whom perfection does not exclude simplicity. In a period when Italian painting embarked on subtle intellectual discourse or the weaving of a decorative pattern of lines, he avoids both. Employing tempera, already superseded by oils that permitted finer chiaroscuro modeling, he presents the traditional image of the Virgin of Humility through the contrast of the tenderest flesh tones, her scarlet blouse and blue cape, echoed by the azure distances beyond the arched windows. Enclosed by masterly drawing in a sculptural form, these resonant colors form an absolute balance of earthly and heavenly.

Leonardo da Vinci. *Madonna with a Flower (Benois Madonna)*. 1478–80. Oil on canvas (transferred from panel). 19 ½ x 12 ½ in. (49.5 x 31.5 cm).

According to one theory, this painting is a political allegory that refers to the events of the Pazzi conspiracy of 1478, a plot that killed Giuliano dei' Medici and nearly cost the life of his brother Lorenzo. The Christ Child's gaze is fixed not on the flower in the Virgin's hand but on the rounded patches of light reflected in the brooch on her breast, possibly an allusion to the *palle*, or balls, in the arms of the Medici family.

Francesco Melzi. *Flora*. Between 1510 and 1515. Oil on canvas. 30 x 24 ⅞ in. (76 x 63 cm).
The model for this painting, thought to have been painted by Leonardo da Vinci in the second half of the 15th century, was believed to be a lady from the retinue of King Francis I, the genius's last patron. It is now known to have been painted by his favorite pupil, who depicted Flora, the ancient goddess of vegetation, with flowers executed with the pedantic precision characteristic of Leonardo's school. Included are symbolic flowers: fragrant jasmine in the right hand speaks of lost chastity; the columbine on which the goddess gazes and her bared breast represent fertility; and the anemones in her lap indicate a return to new life.

ABOVE
Raphael (Raffaello Santi). *The Conestabile Madonna*. 1502–3. Tempera on canvas (transferred from panel).
6 ⅞ x 7 in. (17.5 x 18 cm).
Restoration of this tondo revealed that Raphael originally showed the Virgin holding a pomegranate and not a book.
This painting forms a cohesive whole with the frame, which was made to the artist's design. He likely painted this work
before moving to Florence in 1504, perhaps to a commission from the Perugian noble Alfani Diamante (the work is
mentioned in family property inventories in 1660 and 1665). In the 18th century the Alfanis became related to the
Conestabile family. It was from Count Scipione Conestabile that Alexander II bought the painting in 1871.

OPPOSITE
Raphael (Raffaello Santi). *The Holy Family (Madonna with the Beardless Joseph)*. 1506. Oil and tempera on canvas
(transferred from panel). 28 ½ x 22 ½ in. (72.5 x 57 cm).
The way Joseph is depicted in this work, distinctly individual and unusual for the iconography of the saint, gave rise to
suggestions that Raphael depicted one of his own contemporaries. More likely, he was inspired by the depictions of old
men produced by Leonardo da Vinci.

ABOVE

Giulio Romano (Giulio Pippi). *Love Scene*. 1524–26. Oil on canvas. 64 ⅛ x 132 ⅜ in. (163 x 337 cm).
Because of its purportedly indecent subject, this painting was not included in the Hermitage's catalogues until the 20th
century, even though it had entered the collection in the 1780s. It may show the encounter between Zeus and Alcmene:
the alarmed dog at the maidservant's feet points to a breach of marital fidelity. The bed's carved decoration of a satyr
and nymph may allude to another of Zeus's amorous adventures, when he assumed the guise of a satyr to make love
to the nymph Antiope.

P. 156
Andrea del Sarto (Andrea Domenico d'Agnolo). *Madonna and Child with St. Catherine, St. Elizabeth, and St. John the Baptist.* 1510s. Oil on canvas. 40 ⅛ x 31 ½ in. (102 x 80 cm).
Andrea del Sarto, a pupil of Fra Bartolommeo, was the most significant representative of the Florentine school in the early decades of the 16th century and taught several outstanding Mannerist painters, including Rosso Fiorentino, Pontormo, and Bronzino. This work was painted as an altarpiece. According to one theory, the model for St. Catherine may have been Lucrezia del Fede, the artist's wife.

ABOVE

Francesco Francia (Francesco di Marco di Giacomo Raibolini). *The Virgin and the Child with St. Lawrence and St. Jerome and Two Angels Making Music*. 1500. Tempera and oil on canvas (transferred from panel). 76 x 59 ½ in. (193 x 151 cm).

A mixture of influences—the Gothically dry painting of Ferrara, the Umbrian pursuit of soft singing lines, and Venetian coloristic refinement—led the Bolognese Francia to the "sweetness and harmony of paints" that Vasari noted. The artist was famed no less as an engraver, medallist, and goldsmith than as a painter. The inscription on the throne reads, "Signor Ludovico Calcina . . . , canon of San Petronio in Bologna, the reviver and creator, founder and restorer of that church [for which the painting was made] valued me, Francia the goldsmith, highly. Bologna. 1500."

ABOVE

Bernardino Fungai. *The Magnanimity of Scipio Africanus*. Oil and tempera on panel. 24 ½ x 65 ⅜ in. (62 x 166 cm). The subject on this panel from a *cassone* (wedding chest) was popular in the Renaissance era. Bernardino Fungai combines three successive episodes in Livy's account of the hero's irreproachable treatment of the vanquished during the Second Punic War. Soldiers in the right-hand portion are shown bringing a beautiful female prisoner as a gift to Scipio. Upon learning that the girl was betrothed, Scipio returned her to her parents and fiancé. The couple who commissioned the painting may have wanted to hold up Scipio as an example to their son-in-law.

Alessandro Allori. *Allegory of the Christian Church*. Early 1600s. Oil on canvas. 51 ½ x 45 ¼ in. (131 x 115 cm).
It is no easy matter to identify the beautiful, golden-haired Florentine woman wreathed with flowers like Flora or Spring as the Christian Church, or the boy with a languishing satiated look as Christ, betrothing himself to her and rejecting the Synagogue. In the interpretation of Allori, a late Mannerist who worked (among other things) on the murals in the Studiolo of Francis I Medici in the Palazzo Vecchio, the pious subject acquired a strong character of courtly romance.

Correggio (Antonio Allegri). *Female Portrait*. Ca. 1518. Oil on canvas. 40 ½ x 34 ½ in. (103 x 87.5 cm).
Among those purported to be the subject of this portrait is the notorious poisoner Lucretia Borgia and Salome, the legendary step-daughter of Herod Antipas, among others. A better-founded but still speculative interpretation is that she is the poet Veronica Gambara (1485–1550), who ruled the principality of Correggio after the death of her husband, Giberto X, in 1518. The laurel tree symbolizes the model's poetic gifts, and the ivy indicates her married (widowed) status.

Agnolo Bronzino (?). *Portrait of Cosimo I Medici*. 1537. Oil on canvas.
46 ¼ x 34 ½ in. (117.5 x 87.5 cm).

This portrait is full of allegorical attributes that refer to Cosimo I Medici (1519–74) and convey a message of a positive destiny, power, and fame. The medal bears a winged female figure supported by two spheres—an embodiment of Cosmography (the science studying the universe's structure) and, for contemporaries, an obvious reference to Cosimo. Also featured are the balls from the Medici arms. The fire in the depths of the painting symbolizes both God's providence and the desire for glory and action.

Jacopo Pontormo (Jacopo Carrucci). *Madonna and Child with St. Joseph and John the Baptist*. 1520s. Oil on canvas. 47 ¼ x 38 ¾ in. (120 x 98.5 cm).

In this superb example of Pontormo's style, the theme of a premonition of the predestined Passion grows smoothly from the center to the edges and from the surface into the depths. From the infant amusing himself with a young goldfinch, our gaze shifts to the Virgin's sad face, then to the resigned faces of Joseph and John the Baptist, before finally plunging into the agitated gloom of the firmament, in front of which the ominous cross looms.

OPPOSITE

Giorgione (Giorgio Barbarelli da Castelfranco) (?). *The Virgin and Child in a Landscape*. Ca. 1503. Oil on canvas (transferred from panel). 17 ⅜ x 14 ⅜ in. (44 x 36.5 cm).

Just a century prior to this painting's creation, Venetian painting knew nothing of space and remained true to the Byzantine convention of golden backgrounds. The innovations of Giovanni Bellini, in whose work the landscape became visual testimony to the grandeur of the world God created, were already being skillfully developed in the early works of his pupil Giorgione. Chromatically more resonant and enriched by contrasts of light and shade, this landscape sets the tone and gives the Christian subject a new, sensual-poetic content.

RIGHT

Giorgione (Giorgio Barbarelli da Castelfranco). *Judith*. Ca. 1504. Oil on canvas (transferred from panel). 56 ⅝ x 26 ⅛ in. (144 x 66.5 cm).

Created by Giorgione at about age 26, this painting is one of the few reliably attributed to the artist. It is marked by exceptional skill in the drawing and use of color as well as by a youthfully playful approach to the Old Testament legend. Giorgione depicts the courageous widow, who saved her city from Assyrian invaders by decapitating their commander Holofernes, in the guise of an enchanting girl whose true weapon is not her sword but her beauty.

PP. 166–167

Titian (Tiziano Vecellio). *Danaë*. Ca. 1554. Oil on canvas. 47 ¼ x 73 ⅝ in. (120 x 187 cm).

According to *The Amours of Jupiter*, the mythical king Acrisius was scared by an oracle predicting his death at the hands of a son born to his daughter Danaë, so he promptly locked her in a tower. Jupiter fell in love with the maiden, turning into a golden shower to reach her. Titian shows the heat of passion by dividing the painting in two: on the right, the servant catches gold coins in her skirt, while on the left, Danaë's body reigns.

Bonifazio Veronese (Bonifazio de Pitati). *Portrait of a Young Man.* 1510s. Oil on canvas (transferred from panel). 18 ⅞ x 15 in. (48 x 38 cm).
The soft shape of the face, the rhythm of rounded lines forming a simple balanced composition, the man's thoughtful look seemingly detached from earthly realities— these elements speak of the influence of Giorgione, who ruled the minds of Venetian artists in the first half of the 16th century. This portrait has been attributed to Vincenzo Catena, Giovanni Cariani, Lorenzo Lotto, and others but is now considered one of Bonifazio Veronese's few ventures into this genre.

Titian (Tiziano Vecellio). *Portrait of a Young Woman.* Ca. 1536. Oil on canvas. 37 ¾ x 29 ½ in. (96 x 75 cm).
The crispness and precision of the contours in this portrait, unusual for the mature Titian, have caused specialists to doubt its current attribution. But the refined eroticism is typical of an artist who several times depicted Venuses uninhibitedly demonstrating their nakedness in the setting of a rich Italian house. Here, he does without mythological pretext; the beautiful model has even been perceived as the celebrated patroness of the arts Eleonora Gonzaga, the wife of the Duke of Urbino.

Paolo Veronese (Paolo Cagliari). *The Adoration of the Magi.* Early 1570s. Oil on copper.
17 ¾ x 13 ½ in. (45 x 34.5 cm).

Sumptuous fabrics, Eastern costumes, outlandish animals—all the typical attributes of medieval and Renaissance compositions of the Adoration of the Magi—were known to Veronese not just from his predecessors' works. Venice in its golden age was Europe's richest commercial port and abounded in exotica. In Veronese's painting, its joyous motley was reflected more brightly than in the works of his great contemporaries, Titian, Tintoretto, and the rest: It passed directly into his palette.

ABOVE

Titian (Tiziano Vecellio). *The Repentant Mary Magdalene.* 1560s. Oil on canvas.
46 ⅞ x 38 ⅛ in. (119 x 97 cm).

The tense gloomy color scheme conveys the confusion of emotions that accompany repentance, but Titian invests the image of the Magdalene with a certain ambiguity. The impulse to prayer makes the girl particularly beautiful, conveying the impression that acknowledgment of sin and approaching retribution is a vital condition for the blooming of the flesh.

Jacopo Tintoretto (Jacopo Robusti). *The Nativity of John the Baptist.* Ca. 1550. Oil on canvas. 71 ¼ x 104 ¾ in. (181 x 266 cm).

Tintoretto's oeuvre is marked by a keen sense of chaos. In any subject he finds action, and in any action he finds many disconnected actions. This is true of his account of John the Baptist's nativity, which becomes an eloquent depiction of the turmoil reigning in any home at the birth of a child. The saint's mother, Elizabeth, recuperates on the bed and the Virgin Mary holds the newborn as his father recovers the power of speech, in accordance with the prophecy.

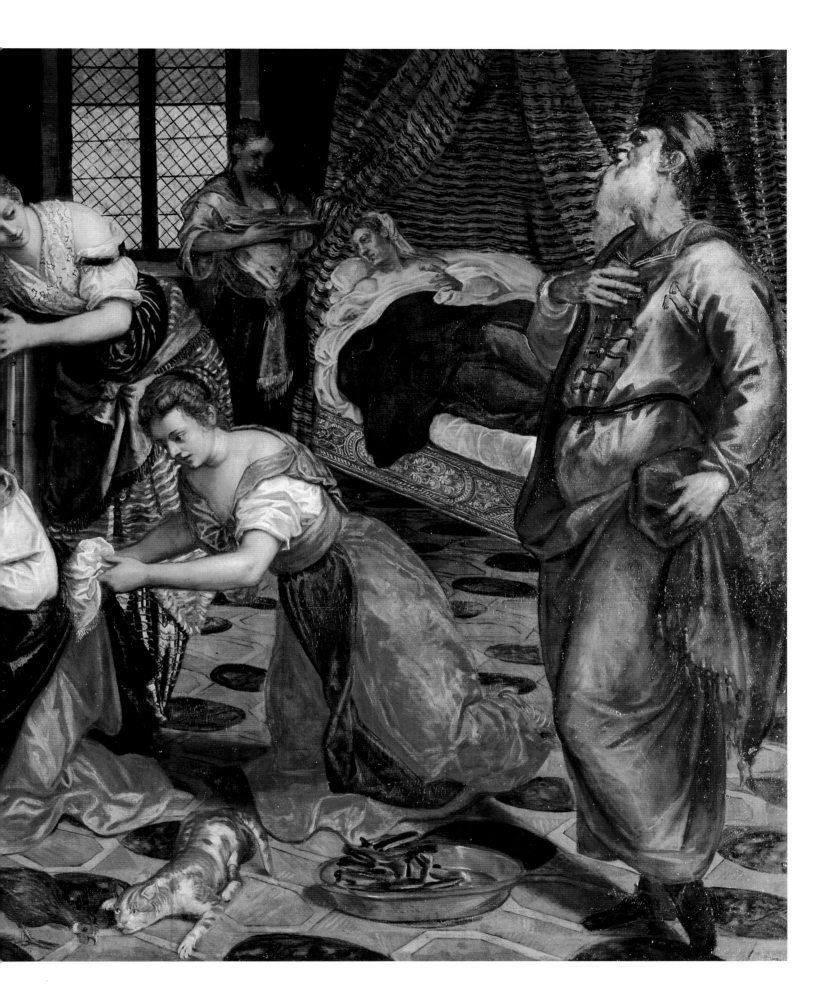

Paolo Veronese (Paolo Cagliari). *The Lamentation*. Between 1576 and 1582. Oil on canvas. 57 ⅞ x 43 ⅞ in. (147 x 111.5 cm).

In this relatively small composition, Veronese uses devices tried and tested in his monumental multifigure canvases: a low viewpoint, mighty vertical arcs determining the placement of figures, and a sweeping gesture that stretches the painting toward the viewer. His *Lamentation* is the opposite of Titian's heart-rending *Pietà* of the same period (Accademia, Venice). It comes across more as a bright prelude to the triumph of the Resurrection, and, as ever, the characteristic combination of pure, rather cold tones delights the eye.

Titian (Tiziano Vecellio). *St. Sebastian*. Ca. 1570. Oil on canvas. 82 ⅝ x 45 ¼ in. (210 x 115 cm).

The flesh remained one of the main objects of Titian's reflections even in the last years of his life. Here, it is no longer the regal flesh of Venus or Danaë but rather the suffering flesh of the martyr that at the same time rejects suffering. It is filled not with greatness but with strength, and that strength is expressed directly, by the flesh of the painting itself. *St. Sebastian* is undoubtedly beautiful, but it is the beauty of torment.

ABOVE

Lorenzo Lotto. *Family Portrait*. 1523/24. Oil on canvas. 37 ¾ x 45 ⅝ in. (96 x 116 cm).
The dog symbolizes faithfulness and constancy, whereas the Latin inscription reads
HOMO NUNQUAM, or "A man never." (The probable continuation is "behaves like a male
squirrel," an animal that, so it was believed in the Middle Ages, drove the female from
the dray in winter to avoid sharing his store of food.) The old-fashioned attributes and
overt posing of the couple do not interfere with the portrait's astonishing naturalness,
achieved thanks to Lotto's relaxed and ironic eye.

Caravaggio (Michelangelo Merisi da Caravaggio). *The Lute Player*. Ca. 1595.
Oil on canvas. 37 x 61 ⅜ in. (94 x 119 cm).

The crack in the lute, the damaged pear, the music of a madrigal well known at the end
of the 16th century, and the musician's sad look leave no doubt that this painting is an
allegory of unrequited love. At the same time, the strong chiaroscuro and tangible
materiality of the still life, so abundant and carefully executed, are clear testimony to the
original style and uncompromising character of the 22-year-old Caravaggio.

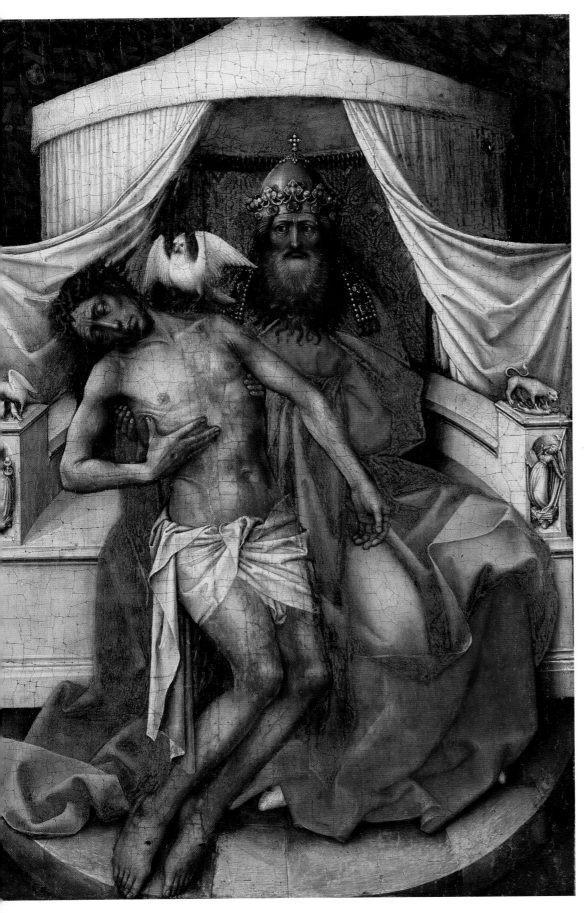

Robert Campin. *The Holy Trinity. Virgin and Child by the Fireplace*. Diptych. 1430s. Oil on panel. Each panel 13 ½ x 9 ⅝ in. (34.3 x 24.5 cm).

This work, one of the best by the Master of Flémalle, demonstrates the tendencies and peculiarities of a transitional period in Netherlandish art, when traditions derived from icon painting quaintly combine with realistic innovations. It is fairly stylized, whereas the depiction of the Virgin is reminiscent of a genre scene set in a 15th-century burgher's dwelling. It abounds in details included not just for their symbolic meaning but also because of the artist's interest in conveying the material and texture of objects.

ABOVE

Geertgen tot Sint Jans (?). *St. Bavo.* Last third of the 15th century. Oil on canvas. 14 ⅜ x 11 ⅞ in. (36.5 x 30 cm).

Bavo, a knight and landowner who at the end of his life distributed his wealth to the poor and took monastic vows, is the patron saint of several Low Country cities, including Haarlem, where Geertgen tot Sint Jans worked. Geertgen was one of the first artists in the Netherlands to show a particular interest in landscape, and in the depths of this work's simple unspectacular background we see a church, possibly one of the cathedrals dedicated to the saint.

Rogier van der Weyden. *St. Luke Drawing the Virgin*. 1430s. Oil on canvas (transferred from panel). 40 ⅜ x 42 ¾ in. (102.5 x 108.5 cm).

The subject is based on the apocryphal legend that St. Luke painted the likeness of the Virgin Mary, who appeared to him in a vision. Depicted in the background are Mary's parents, Joachim and Anne. The evangelist, who supposedly practiced medicine, is shown dressed like a Flemish doctor; in the Middle Ages he was considered the patron saint of painters, physicians, and apothecaries. It has been suggested that this is a self-portrait. The way in which Luke holds the stylus resembles the technique artists used to avoid smudging drawings with the heel of the hand.

PP. 182–183

Hugo van der Goes (?). *The Adoration of the Magi*. Late 15th century. Oil on canvas (transferred from panel). 38 x 30 ½ in. (96.3 x 77.5 cm), center; 37 ⅞ x 14 ½ in. (96.2 x 37 cm), wings.

Deviations from established depictions can be found in the central scene, which takes place beneath a canopy in the ruins of David's palace. In the depths to the right is the traditional stall with an ox and ass, although the appearances of the Magi are not canonical. Melchior, who was grey-bearded according to the *Golden Legend* (a medieval collection of apocryphal tales), is here clean-shaven. The usually mature Balthasar is shown as a young Ethiopian, and the young Caspar has been given a beard and long hair.

LEFT

Pieter Coeck van Aalst. *The Agony in the Garden.* 1527–30. Oil on canvas. 32 ⅝ x 22 ¼ in. (83 x 56.5 cm).
Before the arrival of the soldiers brought by Judas to place Christ under arrest, he must complete his prayer and awaken the apostles. Curiously, as a consequence of the artist's pursuit of verisimilitude in depicting the sequence, setting, and details of the Gospel story, the cup—a figure of speech in Christ's appeal to God—has become material in the form of a monument erected on the top of the hill.

OPPOSITE

Jan Provost. *The Virgin in Glory.* 1524. Oil on canvas (transferred from panel). 80 x 59 ½ in. (203 x 151 cm).
Provost remained largely loyal to Gothic art. This altarpiece is filled with figures and objects that form a complex network of biblical allusions. Glory is represented by the mandorla, the radiant aureola surrounding the Mother of God, who stands on a moon and clouds separating the earthly and heavenly worlds. Angels praise her with music echoed below by King David, the composer of psalms. In the center and on the sides are sibyls. The figures are conventional, but the landscape is painted in perspective. Depth is permitted only in the earthly part, while the heavens remain symbolically flat.

Lucas van Leyden. *The Healing of the Blind Man of Jericho.* 1531. Oil on canvas. 45 ½ x 85 ½ in. (115.7 x 217.3 cm).
The combination of rigid, engraving-like drawing and efforts to convey the figures' complex natural movements points to
the influence of German art, above all Dürer. The bustle of a fairground enters into the Gospel scene, while the niches
in the side wings, formerly reserved for saints, are occupied by sumptuously clothed and artistically posed heralds bearing
the arms of the donors, who commissioned the triptych not for a church but, it is believed, for the Leyden city hospital.

P. 188 TOP
Master of the Female Half-Lengths. *The Virgin and Child*. First half of the 16th century.
Oil on panel. 21 x 16 ⅝ in. (53.2 x 42.4 cm).
The contents of the dish toward which Jesus reaches are symbolically significant: grapes represent Christ's earthly nature and his death on the cross for the redemption of human sins, and cherries stand for the Resurrection and the promise of paradise for righteous Christians. Behind Mary's back lies an authentic and expressive Netherlandish landscape, with thatched cottages, a village square and mill, a bird trap, a horseman, an old man carrying a child on his shoulders, and a woman washing laundry in a river.

BELOW

Joachim Patinir (?). *Landscape with the Rest on the Flight into Egypt.* Ca. 1524. Oil on panel. 20 x 37 ¾ in. (51 x 96 cm). The gradual separation of landscape within painting began in the Low Countries in the early 16th century. Albrecht Dürer met Patinir during his journey to Flanders and called him "the good landscape painter," thus giving a name to the genre. But a narrative, most commonly biblical, remained a necessary component of such works for some time. Here, the rural European view is populated by Gospel personages and peasants of the artist's own era, although it is no easy matter to tell them apart.

Master of the Female Half-Lengths. *Female Musicians*. First half of the 16th century. Oil on panel. 21 x 14 ¾ in. (53.2 x 37.5 cm).

At the turn of the 16th century, burgeoning Antwerp became the chief artistic center of the whole of Northern Europe. One of the artists who worked for the city's rich burghers has become known as the "Master of the Female Half-Lengths" on the basis of a group of closely connected works. This scene depicting ladies making music — a kind of love allegory — includes the score of a chanson by Claudin de Sermisy, who composed music at the French court.

Marinus van Roymerswaele. *Tax-Collectors*. Oil on canvas (transferred from panel). 33 ¼ x 23 ⅝ in. (84.5 x 60 cm).
Genre compositions depicting moneychangers, usurers, or merchants became common in 16th-century Netherlandish painting. In contrast to Quentin Massys, who pioneered the theme, Roymerswaele gives his personages satirically pointed, almost grotesque features. The archaic elements in their dress may have been a traditional indicator of their occupation. The many repetitions of this subject (more than 30 variants are known) indicate that it was popular and in enduring demand.

Dirk Jacobsz. *Group Portrait of the Amsterdam Shooting Corporation*. 1532. Oil on canvas (transferred from panel). 45 ¼ x 63 in. (115 x 160 cm).
This painting is among the earliest group portraits created to adorn the interiors of public buildings. The likenesses of 17 marksmen are arranged mechanically in three rows. Their membership in the corporation—a kind of volunteer militia—is indicated by the red and blue capes. The corporation's badge, an eagle's talon, appears on the cape of one of the front-row figures.

ABOVE

Lambert Lombard. *Self-Portrait*. Oil on canvas. 30 ⅛ x 25 ⅜ in. (76.5 x 64.5 cm).

This artist inspired dithyrambs from both of the great 16th-century historians of art: Giorgio Vasari ("Of all the Flemish artists I have named, none is superior to Lambert Lombard of Liège") and Karel van Mander ("One can confidently rank him among the best Netherlandish painters, past and present"). A painter and poet, archaeologist and antiquarian, and an expert on architecture and perspective, Lombard was the head of a large studio.

OPPOSITE

Ambrosius Holbein. *Portrait of a Young Man*. 1518. Tempera and oil on panel. 17 ⅜ x 12 ¾ in. (44 x 32.5 cm).

As indicated by the Latin inscription in the cartouche that gives the date of the portrait, the subject was 20 years old. The composition, the turn of the figure, and the asymmetrical cropping of the arch give grounds for suggesting that originally this was a double portrait. If customary practice is a guide, the missing part of the painting may have been a depiction of the man's wife or bride-to-be.

PP. 194–195

Peter Brueghel the Younger (?). *Winter Landscape with Skaters and a Bird Snare*. Between 1615 and 1620. Oil on panel. 14 ⅞ x 22 in. (37.8 x 55.7 cm).

The subject of ice skating became common in 17th-century Dutch painting and was most often connected with native proverbs that made carefree sliding over thin ice a metaphor for the insecurity of human existence. People who fail to think about this are no cleverer than the birds that fail to notice the trap set for them. This work is a copy of a 1565 original by Peter Brueghel the Elder, one of the first secular paintings produced in the Low Countries.

Master of the Thuison Altarpiece. *The Entry into Jerusalem*. 15th century. Oil on panel. 45 ⅞ x 20 ¼ in. (116.5 x 51.5 cm). According to the Gospels, a week before Christ's death he entered Jerusalem with the apostles, riding like a king, but on a donkey as a sign of humility. The palm leaves with which people greeted him became Christian symbols of martyrdom and victory over death. This painting, which abounds in details of a medieval city, is one panel of a large altarpiece. It follows the late Gothic tradition and resembles a book miniature and 15th-century Netherlandish painting.

Lucas Cranach the Elder. *Virgin and Child under the Apple Tree*. Ca. 1530. Oil on canvas (transferred from panel). 34 ¼ x 23 ¼ in. (87 x 59 cm). The Russian artist and art historian Alexander Benois, an expert on the Hermitage collection, allotted this painting pride of place among the museum's works by Cranach, describing the Virgin's appearance here as "strange, not beautiful yet at the same time captivating." The depiction of Mary against the background of an apple tree— a symbol of the Fall—stresses her role in the redemption of original sin, while the apple that Christ holds in his left hand points to the coming atonement.

PELLE · CVPIDINEOS · TOTO   CONAMINE · LVXVS
NE · TVA · POSSIDEAT   PECTORA · CECA · VE

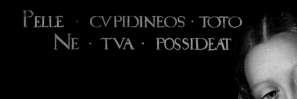

LEFT
Lucas Cranach the Elder. *Venus and Cupid*. 1509. Oil on canvas (transferred from panel). 83 ⅞ x 40 ⅛ in. (213 x 102 cm).
This painting is the first depiction of a naked Venus in German art. The interest in mythology, which often served as a pretext for a display of nudity, may have been dictated by humanist fashion. At the same time, Cranach's strict sense of propriety caused him to accompany the depiction with a moralizing Latin couplet: "Reject Cupid's lasciviousness with all your might, or else Venus will possess your blinded soul."

OPPOSITE
Lucas Cranach the Elder. *Portrait of a Woman*. 1526. Oil on panel. 34 ⅞ x 23 in. (88.5 x 58.5 cm).
Cranach's brush is devoid of tenderness and more closely resembles an engraver's burin. His color scheme is founded on simple combinations of local colors, and, although he had mastered Renaissance illusionism, he was in no hurry to abandon stiff Gothic outlines. Yet no small part of his income came from courtly scenes with nude figures and portraits of beauties like this one, so his devotion to a painting style that seems alien to eroticism might be regarded as calculation that paid off.

Pierre Dumoustier the Elder. *Portrait of a Youth*. Between 1570 and 1575. Oil on canvas. 12 ½ x 7 ½ in. (32 x 19 cm). Dumoustier was a famous portraitist and creator of virtuoso drawings (which can also be found in the Hermitage). In this portrait he demonstrates an astonishing freedom, preferring simplicity and faithfulness to the model over idealization, and makes no effort to conceal his rapid painting manner. The resulting impression of freshness and modernity is intensified by the audacious composition, with its cut-off edges.

Corneille de Lyon. *Portrait of a Woman*. 1530s. Oil on panel. 7 ⅞ x 6 ⅛ in. (20 x 15.5 cm).
The French Renaissance was much assisted by the Italian enthusiasms of King Francis I (r. 1515–47), who during three invasions of the peninsula established contacts with artists and poets; it expressed itself primarily in a blossoming of portrait painting. Young aristocrats increasingly commissioned likenesses of their sweethearts, demanding that artists observe not so much upper-class decorum as vivid naturalness. The miniature portraits of Corneille de Lyon, a native of Flanders, illustrate this tendency.

Unknown Spanish Master of the 15th-Century Castilian School (Circle of Sancho de Zamora?). *The Entombment*. Tempera and oil on panel. 37 x 76 ⅜ in. (94 x 194 cm).

The Gothic conventionality of this painting's composition did not hinder the artist from investing it with an exceptional keenness of feelings—religious as well as broader human ones. The piercingly bright stripe of blood stretching along Christ's pale body repeats and emphasizes the lifeless fracture of its lines. The color is echoed by the clothing of the mourners and flowers, whose expressiveness is far from symbolic. The donor who commissioned the painting for a church is shown below, by the coffin.

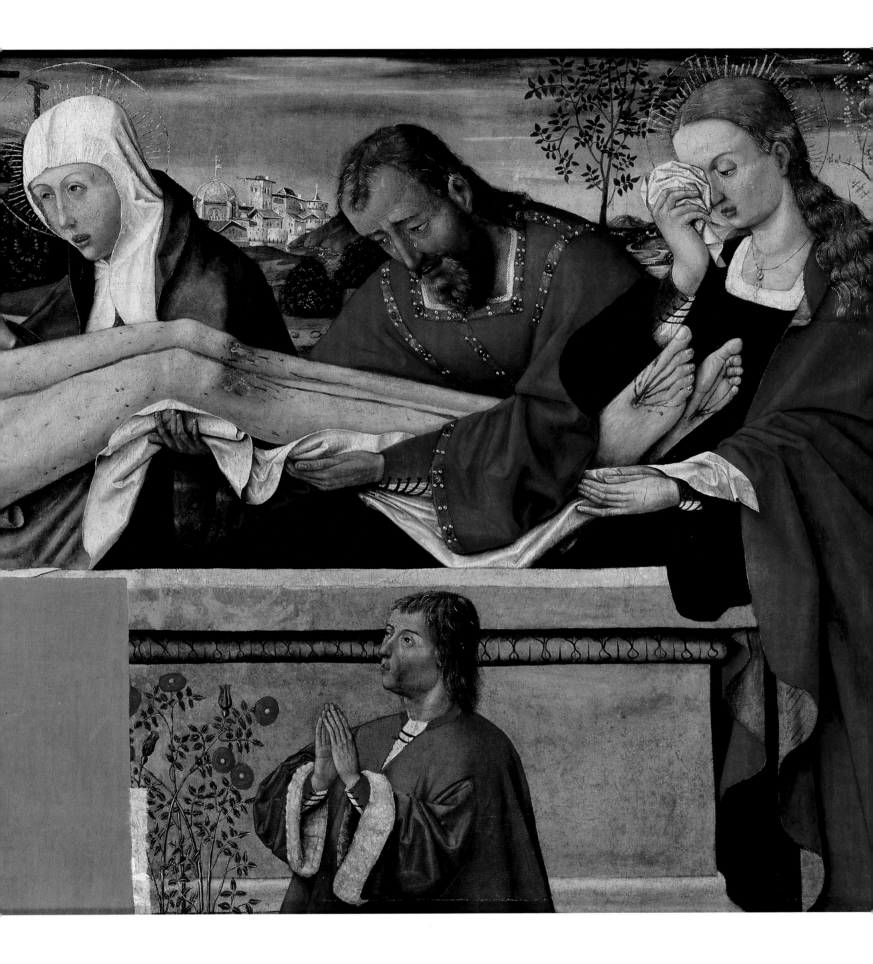

El Greco (Domenicos Theotocopoulos). *The Apostles Peter and Paul*. Between 1587 and 1592.
Oil on canvas. 47 ⅞ x 41 ⅜ in. (121.5 x 105 cm).
The intensive colors of the cloaks, whose energy underlines the Baroque contrasts of light and shade, did not prevent El Greco from creating a balanced composition. The delicate painting of the hands and portrait-like faces concentrate the attention on the humanity of Peter and Paul (the latter resembles El Greco), while the freely executed patches of clothing give a sense of the greatness of the apostles' ministry. This combination demonstrates the possibilities of depicting such spiritual matters as humility and obsession.

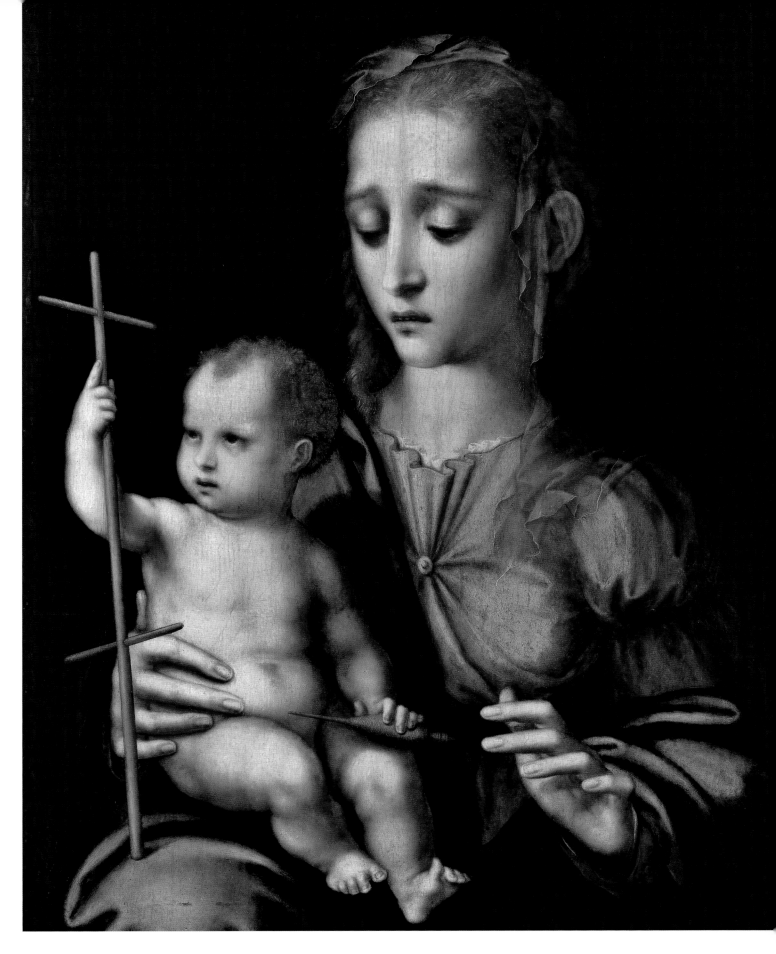

Luis de Morales. *The Virgin and Child*. 1570s. Oil on canvas (transferred from panel). 28 ⅛ x 20 ½ in. (71.5 x 52 cm).
In Morales's work Spanish Gothic traditions blend fancifully with Netherlandish and Italian influences. The depiction
of the Virgin with a cross-shaped distaff—an attribute of Mary's everyday occupations that also points to the future
Calvary—can be found in the work of Leonardo da Vinci and his pupils. The latter's soft and sentimental manner,
with its tendency toward linear decorativeness, has an opposite effect here, proving to be in harmony with profound
religious feeling.

ABOVE
Francisco de Zurbarán. *The Girlhood of the Virgin*. Ca. 1660. Oil on canvas. 29 x 21 in. (73.5 x 53.5 cm).
Zurbarán's exalted and naïve piety and his close affinity with popular culture expressed themselves in his amazing
gift as a colorist. The pure, bright, intensive hues of his paintings, most often dictated by Christian symbolism,
seem automatically combined, yet they come together in unexpected poignant harmonies. Here, the red of Mary's
dress signifies love and charity; the white of the stitching purity and innocence; the green, youth and the enclosed
garden of paradise, one more symbol of immaculacy.

Francisco de Zurbarán. *St. Lawrence*. 1636. Oil on canvas. 115 x 88 ½ in. (292 x 225 cm).
In contrast to other geniuses of the Spanish golden age, Zurbarán appears modest, lacking their boldness of innovative approaches and technical virtuosity. But he was far more strongly connected with traditional Spanish piety, with its ardor and tendency to mysticism. Acclaimed by his contemporaries, he executed many commissions for monastery buildings. The Monastery of San José was the source of this large image of St. Lawrence shown in deacon's vestments and the instrument of his martyrdom, the gridiron on which he was said to have been roasted alive.

ABOVE
Juan Pantoja de la Cruz. *Portrait of Diego de Villamayor*. 1605. Oil on canvas. 35 x 28 in. (89 x 71 cm).
Like El Greco, Pantoja de la Cruz was familiar with the work of Venetian painters and even copied Titian's *Portrait of Charles V* for the Escorial, but he took from them only the impressive pose of the formal portrait and avoided the expression of feelings and emotions. The main element in this portrait of a prominent aristocrat is the armor, which allows us to judge the skill and style of Spanish armorers, who found inspiration in Moorish ornament.

Diego Velázquez. *Portrait of Don Gaspar de Guzman y Pimental, Count-Duke of Olivares*. Ca. 1638. Oil on canvas. 26 ⅜ x 21 ½ in. (67 x 54.5 cm).

This prime minister of Philip IV began his career with a dizzying rise and ended it with a no-less-vertiginous fall, spending his last years in exile. When his star was ascending he introduced the young Velázquez to the king, and the artist painted his powerful patron several times. In this portrait, made shortly before Olivares suffered a series of defeats in both his foreign policy projects and court intrigues, his face clearly betrays fatigue and disillusionment.

Diego Velázquez. *Breakfast*. Ca. 1617. Oil on canvas. 42 ¾ x 40 ⅛ in.
(108.5 x 102 cm).
The fashion for depicting common people ushered in by Caravaggio spread across
the whole of western Europe in the early 1600s. Scenes set in inns became popular
in Spain and were often commissioned as signs. Such works are known as *bodegones*,
from the Spanish word for "tavern." Working in this genre the 18-year-old Velázquez
demonstrates a mastery of line and chiaroscuro modelling, while his cold manner,
avoiding amusement and any hint of drama, gives significance to this scene of daily life.

Bartolomé Esteban Murillo. *Boy with a Dog*. Between 1655 and 1660. Oil on canvas. 27 ½ x 23 ⅜ in. (70 x 60 cm).

The young Murillo first made his name with small genre scenes from the life of simple urban folk and homeless children, painted at a time when a plague was raging in his native Seville. His works are always full of a natural realism free of ideological content. By the end of the 1640s, after he had traveled to Madrid and become acquainted with the painting of Velázquez and Venetian artists, his use of chiaroscuro grew finer and his compositions acquired a more stylized and sentimental character.

LEFT
Alonso Cano. *The Crucifixion.*
Ca. 1636–38, Oil on canvas.
104 ⅜ x 68 ⅛ in. (265 x 173 cm).
Compositionally pared down Crucifixion
scenes that differ from the theatrical
scenes of the Middle Ages and
Renaissance, with their abundance of
action and detail, were frequently
commissioned after the Council of Trent
(1545–63), whose resolutions were aimed
at strengthening Catholic morality and
faith; they became especially common in
Spain. This large altarpiece, apparently
painted for a Dominican monastery, is
intended to be viewed from below and to
encourage prayerful concentration.

OPPOSITE
Bartolomé Esteban Murillo.
The ("Walpole") Immaculate Conception.
1680. Oil on canvas. 76 ¾ x 57 in.
(195 x 145 cm).
In his mature religious canvases Murillo
follows schemes tried and tested by his
predecessors, including those for the
Immaculate Conception. Here the
Mother of God is depicted in heaven,
surrounded by angels and transfused by
divine light. The typical Baroque
dynamic movement and expressive use of
light and shade are coupled with a note of
tender joy that brought the artist broad
approbation.

PP. 214–215
Bernardo Strozzi. *The Healing of Tobit*. Ca. 1635. Oil on canvas. 62 ¼ x 88 in. (158 x 223.5 cm).
Gathered around Tobit are the key figures of the Old Testament account of his life: his wife, Anna; their son Tobias; the loyal dog that accompanied Tobias and the angel on their dangerous journey; and the fish that nearly killed Tobias before he caught it and removed its organs to make a medicine to restore his father's eyesight. For Strozzi the main means of expression is color, so bright and rich compared to his other paintings that it seems an eloquent metaphor for the end to the old man's blindness.

Peter Paul Rubens. *The Descent from the Cross*. Ca. 1617–18. Oil on canvas. 117 x 78 ¾ in. (297 x 200 cm).
After the success of the altar triptych on this subject that Rubens painted for the Antwerp cathedral in 1612, he produced several variants, with his pupils, for different churches. In this one, which adorned the Capuchin church in Lierre, the composition has undergone significant changes. The artist reduced the number of figures and increased the scale of Christ, focusing all the attention on his body and the kinsfolk and disciples, who do not so much support him as simply touch his body.

Peter Paul Rubens. *Portrait of a Lady-in-Waiting to the Infanta Isabella*. Mid-1620s. Oil on panel.
25 ⅛ x 18 ⅞ in. (64 x 48 cm).
Lady-in-Waiting to the Infanta Isabella is the title given to a similar girl whom Rubens depicted in a 1623 drawing now in the Albertina in Vienna. Yet the hairstyle, facial expression, and reserved smile link the figure in both works to likenesses of the artist's daughter, Clara Serena (1611–23). Rubens restrains his explosive temperament and (rare for him) paints not the flesh but the feeling, finding the finest nuances of his favorite colors: red in the girl's face, golden ochre in the hair, and lapis lazuli in the lace.

Peter Paul Rubens. *The Union of Earth and Water*. Ca. 1618. Oil on canvas. 87 ½ x 71 in. (222.5 x 180.5 cm).
The painting's present title was given in the late 19th century by analogy with other allegories of Antwerp and its river, the Scheldt, which allowed the city to flourish by giving it access to the sea. Antwerp is here depicted as the mother goddess Cybele, the Scheldt as Neptune. But we may interpret the reference as being the union of two elements. The main point in Rubens's allegories is not the attributes and meanings. Written sources describe the city's history far better, but without his paintings the spirit of Flanders when it flourished for the last time is incomprehensible.

Peter Paul Rubens. *Bacchus*. Between 1638 and 1640. Oil on canvas. 75 ⅛ x 63 ½ in. (191 x 161.3 cm).
In Rubens's oeuvre, northern European traditions are depicted similarly to ancient and Renaissance prototypes. A corpulent Bacchus—dissimilar to the handsome youth of the ancient Romans and Italians—is often featured in Low Country engravings devoted to the seasons. Although in that context the god's image is invested with a warning against overindulgence and complacency, here his gigantic figure is perceived as a hymn to the earthy joys of the flesh, and the wine brimming over as sap feeding nature's eternal cycle.

S. Thomas Wharton brother
to Philip now Lord Wharton
1639 about y' age of 25.

S' Ant: Vandik

PP. 220–221

Peter Paul Rubens. *The Stone Haulers.* Ca. 1620. Oil on canvas (transferred from panel). 33 ⅞ x 49 ⅞ in. (86 x 126.5 cm).

Rubens generally painted his landscapes for himself. That explains not only the lack of his pupils' involvement and a biblical or mythological basis in such works but also their experimental nature. Here Rubens depicts a moonlit night and a day, with the central foreground scene brightly lit by some third source. Along with the terrain heaving in different directions, resisting the haulers' efforts and the dissonant chorus of trees, this imbues the painting with a physical sense of transformation.

LEFT

Anthony van Dyck. *Portrait of Sir Thomas Wharton.* Second half of the 1630s. Oil on canvas. 85 ½ x 50 ½ in. (217 x 128.5 cm).

As court painter to Charles I of England between 1632 and 1641 van Dyck fully revealed his talent for formal portraiture. In his depictions of English aristocrats, the subjects' lofty status and strong qualities are conveyed not just by pose and attributes, but also by purely painterly features: resonant color combinations, exquisite texture, free brushwork. A devotion to a grand style that permitted— and even turned to advantage—an artistically uninhibited manner became, through van Dyck's example, a distinguishing feature of English painting.

ABOVE
Anthony van Dyck. *Self-Portrait*. Ca. 1622–23. Oil on canvas. 45 ⅞ x 36 ⅞ in. (116.5 x 93.5 cm).
After honing his exceptional natural talent in Rubens's studio, in the early 1620s van Dyck began his career as a society portraitist in Genoa, taking commissions from the local aristocracy while studying the legacy of the Renaissance masters. The young artist's haughty pose shows unshakeable self-confidence, which had good foundation: his style was already brilliant, both figuratively and literally. His virtuoso brush invests everything—from the material of the cloak to the glowing youthful skin—with the luster of solid prosperity.

OPPOSITE
Jacob Jordaens. *Self-Portrait with Parents, Brothers, and Sisters.* Ca. 1615. Oil on canvas. 69 x 54 ⅛ in. (175 x 137.5 cm).
In 1616 the 23-year-old Jordaens was accepted into Antwerp's Guild of St. Luke, a corporation of artists. Evidently, to mark the occasion he painted a work that reflects his ebullient artistic temperament and fondness for didactic symbolism. The bread on the table and the wine in the head of the family's glass represent the faith that unites its members; the dog, the strength of marital ties; the lute in the artist's hands, family harmony. The putti hovering above probably stand for three more sisters who died in infancy.

ABOVE
David Teniers the Younger. *Flautist.* Mid-1630s. Oil on canvas. 9 ⅞ x 7 ⅝ in. (25 x 19.5 cm).
In the 1630s the young Teniers was strongly influenced by Adriaen Brouwer, who reintroduced into Flemish painting the practice of depicting common people, begun by the Elder Brueghel. Teniers rapidly moved on from depicting brawls in murky peasant huts and taverns to a sentimental scrutiny of the life of the poor. When he became court painter to the regent, Archduke Leopold William, his exalted patron appreciated such genre scenes as well as his formal portraits and depictions of notable events.

Frans Snyders. *Fish Stall*. Between 1618 and 1621. Oil on canvas. 81 ½ x 134 ¼ in. (207 x 341 cm).

The sinuous lines of fish, familiar from childhood to an artist whose father owned one of Antwerp's biggest eating-houses, seem made for dynamic Baroque compositions. The precision with which Snyders depicts the denizens of seas and rivers delights zoologists, but the abundance of his many *Fish Stalls* is ruled not by any Linnaean hierarchy: the crustaceans whose shedding of their shells symbolized the resurrection are superior to the dead fish.

LEFT

Jacob Jordaens. *The Bean King.*
Ca. 1638. Oil on canvas. 61 ⅞ x 83 in.
(157 x 211 cm).

Jordaens probably depicted his teacher
and father-in-law, Adam van Noort, as
the Bean King, the central figure in the
traditional Low Countries celebration of
Epiphany, who is chosen by finding a
bean baked in a pie. He shows burghers
making merry with evident sympathy,
which brings out the fine line separating
hedonism from moralizing in his
paintings.

ABOVE

Jacob van Oost the Elder. *David with the Head of Goliath*. 1643. Oil on canvas. 40 ⅛ x 32 in. (102 x 81 cm).
When depicting the aftermath of the victory gained by David, the future king of Israel, over the Philistine giant Goliath,
the artist was likely inspired by Caravaggio's work on the same subject. Like the great Italian master, he invested the
scene with almost shocking naturalism, inspiring worldly reflections about the triumph of youth over age, beauty over
ugliness.

OPPOSITE

Rembrandt Harmensz. van Rijn. *The Sacrifice of Isaac*. 1635. Oil on canvas. 76 x 52 in. (193 x 132 cm).
The composition's theatrical dynamics, based on eloquent gestures, link this early but already mature painting
by Rembrandt with the European aesthetics of the Baroque. Between the movements of Abraham's hands (the left
covering his son's face before he kills him; the right stopped at the last moment on God's command) and the angel's
exhorting gesture, a whole spectacle unfolds. It lasts only an instant yet encompasses the brutal collision of faith and
fatherly love.

Rembrandt Harmensz. van Rijn. *The Descent from the Cross*. 1634. Oil on canvas. 62 ¼ x 46 in. (158 x 117 cm).
In 1633 and 1634 Rembrandt produced several painted and etched versions of this subject, reflecting a search for the most expressive arrangement and lighting and his gradual movement away from Rubens's composition. This canvas can be regarded as the final stage of that quest: Rembrandt uses light of varying intensity to pick out not only Christ but also Mary on the right and the women on the left, shifting the sense of tragedy from the event to how those close to Jesus experienced it.

Rembrandt Harmensz. van Rijn. *Flora*. 1634. Oil on canvas. 49 ¼ x 39 ¾ in. (125 x 101 cm).
The 28-year-old Rembrandt depicted his bride, Saskia van Uylenburgh, in the guise of Flora. The flowers that adorn the classical goddess's hair and twine around her staff are almost the only ones in the artist's oeuvre, and although they are painted in a masterly manner, their role remains secondary. Along with the elegantly gleaming fabrics of Saskia's dress, they are details of a spiritual portrait of a young woman.

Rembrandt Harmensz. van Rijn. *The Holy Family*. 1645. Oil on canvas. 46 x 35 ⅞ in. (117 x 91 cm).
Rembrandt depicted the Holy Family often in drawings and paintings, seeking the best composition for a subject that almost literally expresses the idea of Christ's dual human and divine nature. Here the scene takes place in an ordinary Dutch home. The carpenter father is busy at work while the mother watches over her sleeping child. The miracle enters unbeknown to the personages: descending on waves of light, the angel brings down an invisible veil between two worlds, the earthly and the divine.

Rembrandt Harmensz. van Rijn. *Danaë*. 1636. Oil on canvas. 72 ⅞ x 79 ¾ in. (185 x 202.5 cm).
The rendering of mythological and religious subjects in more prosaic imagery, a characteristic of 17th-century Dutch and Flemish painting, led Rembrandt not to a delight in the material richness of the world or the poetry of everyday life, but to the metaphysics of the sublime. Behind the spicy details of one of Jupiter's love affairs, his Danaë addresses the Christian theme of the spiritualization of the flesh: instead of the usual shower of gold, her body is enveloped in a soft light.

Rembrandt Harmensz. van Rijn. *Portrait of the Poet Jeremias de Decker*. 1666. Oil on canvas. 28 x 22 in. (71 x 56 cm). The Hermitage cannot boast even one painted self-portrait by Rembrandt, but this portrait, created shortly before his death, of a friend who knew the artist well seems part of a silent dialogue. Rembrandt depicts himself in the eyes of the other, so fixed and sharp is the poet's gaze, whose depth is intensified by the shadow of the broad brim of a hat that covers half the face.

Rembrandt Harmensz. van Rijn. *Haman Recognizes His Fate*. Ca. 1665. Oil on canvas. 50 x 45 ⅝ in. (127 x 116 cm). Rembrandt's biblical canvases show a search for ways to present the time of the action through the means of painting. From wild Baroque gesticulation he gradually moves to focus on the main elements: composition, lighting, and color. The bloody crimson cloak, the flashes of light on the protagonist's face and hands, and his forward inclination enable us to sense the approach of his life's dramatic end. Whoever he is (doubts remain over the subject), he is directed by divine providence that is indifferent to the fate of the individual yet elevates him as a particle of the Deity.

ABOVE

Rembrandt Harmensz. van Rijn. *Christ and the Samaritan Woman*. 1659. Oil on canvas. 23 ⅝ x 29 ½ in. (60 x 75 cm).
The arc of the colossal vault—a fairly strange architectural top for a well—emerges from the picture toward the viewer
and draws us into the conversation between Christ and the woman, to whom he is explaining his teaching. Words in this
painted sermon are replaced by the ordinary presence of the figures, which Rembrandt achieves through tense nuances
in the use of color, while gestures, facial expressions, and any sort of action take a secondary role.

OPPOSITE

Rembrandt Harmensz. van Rijn. *The Return of the Prodigal Son*. Mid-1660s. Oil on canvas.
103 ⅛ x 80 ¾ in. (262 x 205 cm).
The ending of the Gospel parable of the prodigal son (Luke 15:32) could be the occasion for a dynamic composition.
But Rembrandt confined himself to a single gesture from the father and the reverent gazes of the four observers. The
painting seems an almost literal illustration of the father's admonishment of the indignant older brother ("We had to
celebrate and rejoice, because this brother of yours was dead and has come to life; he was lost and has been found"),
in which Rembrandt hears confirmation that the miracle of resurrection is possible in each human life.

LEFT
Adriaen Brouwer. *Scene in a Tavern (Village Fiddler)*. Between 1634 and 1638. Oil on panel.
9 ⅞ x 13 ⅛ in. (25 x 33.5 cm).
The peasant genre became prevalent in 17th-century Dutch painting. One of its earliest major exponents was Brouwer, who in 1623–24 moved from Flanders to Haarlem, one of many immigrants drawn by the Dutch cities' economic growth. He took up the Netherlandish tradition of depicting scenes from the life of common people that dates back to Pieter Breughel the Elder and Hieronymus Bosch. Here it is enlivened by a taste for everyday details and humor, and the personages have acquired the explosive temperament of the Dutch.

Frans Hals. *Portrait of a Man*. Before 1660. Oil on canvas. 33 ¼ x 26 ⅜ in. (84.5 x 67 cm).
Only the late Hals knew how to preserve the strict precision of a virtuoso painter without keeping his nervous irritation
in check. The almost abstract chromatic perfection does not impede the impression of truthfulness: the white patch
in the foreground, for which it is hard to find an explanation in the subject, emerges from the darkness of the cape with
the same sharpness sensed in the model's arrogant gaze and grumpily crumpled chin.

Gerard Terborch. *Portrait of Catarina van Leunink*. Between 1654 and 1681. Oil on canvas. 31 ½ x 23 ¼ in. (80 x 59 cm).
In the 1640s Terborch developed a type of small full-length portrait with a neutral background and often returned
to it in his late period when depicting wealthy burghers. This model's magnificent dress enabled the artist to demonstrate
his virtuoso skill in conveying fabrics while the subtle color scheme recalls the finest examples of English miniature
portraiture and the gala pictures of van Dyck, with which he had become acquainted in London.

OPPOSITE

Jan Steen. *The Revelers*. Ca. 1660. Oil on panel. 15 ⅜ x 11 ⅞ in. (39 x 30 cm).
The Dutch Revolution of 1568 flung the country into a war with Spain that lasted off and on for 80 years. It was also the start of a stormy economic boom. In Steen's work, this era of euphoria, of daily changes and dangerous temptations, is reflected in an ambiguity that cannot always be resolved. The drunken couple are Steen and his wife, whose disorderly home points out the distressing moral that vice leads to ruin.

ABOVE

Adriaen van Ostade. *A Fight*. 1637. Oil on panel. 9 ⅞ x 13 ⅛ in. (25 x 33.5 cm).
"One hundred Dutchmen, one hundred knives," says one proverb reflecting the quick temper of the inhabitants of Europe's northwestern fringe. In van Ostade's work, this peculiarity of character provided a pretext no worse than a Christian martyrdom or mythological battle for the deployment of typical Baroque devices: dynamic action and dramatic chiaroscuro. Nor did the everyday subject run counter to the period's fondness for allegory, for the painting may have served as a symbolic reference to one of the senses: touch.

ABOVE

Gabriel Metsu. *A Doctor's Visit*. 1660s. Oil on canvas. 24 ¼ x 18 ¾ in. (61.5 x 47.5 cm).
A doctor visiting a sick young woman was a widely used subject in Dutch genre painting. The tendency to allegory
is displayed here, too: the illness is often lovesickness and its undesirable consequences, for which medicine is powerless.
The doctor here is more of a disciplinarian than a healer, and his potions are a moral reproach that is unlikely to aid the
patient but probably acted as a caution to viewers.

ABOVE
Frans Jansz van Mieris the Elder. *Lady at Her Toilette*. Ca. 1659–60. Oil on panel.
20 ¼ x 15 ½ in. (51.5 x 39.5 cm).
The solution to the intrigue suggested by the maid's curious gaze may lie in the objects
on the table: an unsealed letter and the intertwined blue and red ribbons point to the
emotional anxieties of the heroine, who is looking for confirmation of her beloved's
faithfulness.

ABOVE

Gerard Terborch. *Reading a Letter*. Between 1617 and 1681. Oil on canvas. 27 ½ x 21 ¼ in. (70 x 54 cm).
Terborch worked in various Dutch cities and traveled to England, Italy, and Spain, enriching his work with impressions and influences. In the domestic genre scenes of the 1650s and '60s that form the best part of his legacy, there is no pronounced moralizing. On the contrary, the characters, who are often shown in profile or from behind, are engaged in a silent dialogue of looks that allows us only to guess at the meaning of the event.

OPPOSITE

Frans Jansz van Mieris the Elder. *Oyster-Eaters*. 1659. Oil on panel. 17 ½ x 13 ½ in. (44.5 x 34.5 cm).
Mieris's works are marked by the exceptional thoroughness of details, an effective variety of textures, and a smooth manner of painting akin to that of enamel miniatures. The everyday subject has an obvious erotic subtext: the richly furnished interior and elegant attire mask the vice that is cultivated in this establishment dedicated to gratification. The gentleman offers oysters, a symbol of lust and base pleasures. The woman's feigned shyness cannot hide her satiated ennui.

OPPOSITE

Pieter de Hooch (1629–after 1684). *A Woman and Her Maid*. Ca. 1660. Oil on canvas. 20 ⅞ x 16 ½ in. (53 x 42 cm). Despite not belonging to the genre, de Hooch's paintings fit the description of *still life*. Strictly constructed perspective, skillful chiaroscuro, and bright colors create a sense of a frozen moment that encompasses eternity. One of his innovations was the inclusion of adjoining rooms or a street, which not only makes his paintings full of air but also enable us to determine the time and place of their creation. Judging by the canal, this work was painted in Amsterdam after de Hooch's move there in 1661.

ABOVE

Pieter Janssens Elinga. *Room in a Dutch House*. Late 1660s–early 1670s. Oil on canvas. 24 ¼ x 23 ¼ in. (61.5 x 59 cm). The best of Elinga's paintings can be confused with those of Pieter de Hooch, whom he imitated. But his composition is simpler, his line firmer, his shadows sharper, and, most tellingly, he avoided showing faces, whose depiction was often beyond him. Nevertheless, his works have the typical Delft quietness, and their minimalist details and action mean that today's public can hear all the more clearly the rustle of a broom sweeping a stone floor and immerse themselves in the cozy world of a Dutch house.

Jacobus Vrel. *Old Woman by a Fireplace.* 1650s–60s. Oil on canvas. 14 ⅛ x 12 ¼ in. (36 x 31 cm).
Political transformations in 17th-century Holland produced new art customers—ordinary townspeople whose tastes
prompted artists to look closely at simple subjects—and a demand for small paintings to adorn middle-class houses.
Among those artists who accommodated the new artistic audience was Jacobus Vrel, the mysterious "poor man's
Vermeer" (as one critic dubbed him)—either a naïve imitator of the Delft school or, as is suggested by some dated works,
the inventor of the quiet domestic scene that the mid-17th-century genre school then took to perfection.

Emanuel de Witte. *Old Church (Oudekerk) in Delft.* No earlier than 1642. Oil on canvas. 37 ⅜ x 32 ¼ in. (95 x 82 cm).
In his church interiors painted for patrons who built or maintained the buildings, it is hard to find any reflection
of the turbulent life of an artist who was an inveterate gambler with a contentious tendency. De Witte was obliged
to use his paintings to settle his debts; left penniless, he took his own life in despair. His canvases are a complete contrast:
full of majestic calm, a restrained yet resonant harmony, and a neat rhythm despite a complex linear structure.

ABOVE

Pieter Claesz. *Pipes and a Brazier*. 1636. Oil on panel. 19 ¼ x 25 in. (49 x 63.5 cm).
A jug and glass of wine, a snuffbox, pipes, spills, and coals smoldering in a small
brazier—these attributes of the vices of smoking and drunkenness constitute a variant of
the *vanitas*, a still life reminding the viewer of the transience of earthly life. Claesz
supplements the traditional subgenre with an element that increases the eloquence of
the didactic message: the banality of the objects that accompany us on the short journey
from birth to death.

OPPOSITE

Christopher Paudiss. *Still Life*. 1660. Oil on canvas (transferred from panel).
24 ½ x 18 ⅜ in. (62 x 46.5 cm).
German-born Paudiss likely acquired his love of light and ability to depict it in
Rembrandt's studio, where he worked in the early 1640s. His calm light, however,
carries no strong symbolic charge and gives his still lifes, which are devoid of both
triviality and deep significance, the charm of pure art.

LEFT
Willem Claesz Heda. *Breakfast with a Crab.* 1648. Oil on canvas.
46 ½ x 46 ½ in. (118 x 118 cm).
Heda's rich breakfasts bring together, in a refined grey–olive green tone, tokens
of prosperity—silver and gilt tableware, expensive glass articles, and the like. Their
discreet sheen is brought out by the whiteness of the crumpled satin tablecloth,
a symbol of rejected virtue that allows the artist to demonstrate his mastery of
chiaroscuro modeling.

ABOVE
Willem Kalf. *Dessert.* Oil on canvas. 41 ⅜ x 34 ½ in. (105 x 87.5 cm).
Gradually the role of decorativeness expanded in the Dutch still life. Kalf, recognized
as a great artist by contemporaries (rare for exponents of this genre), owed his fame
to the effective combination of a set of elements that appear in different positions
and at different angles in painting after painting: bright yellow and orange fruit,
an oriental carpet with a deep red and black pattern, and exquisitely decorated
tableware that gleams against a dense black background.

Jan Jozefsz van Goyen. *Landscape with an Oak*. 1634. Oil on canvas.
34 ¼ x 41 ⅜ in. (87 x 105 cm).
With Salomon van Ruysdael, van Goyen was a founder of the Haarlem school of Dutch
landscape painting. A tireless draughtsman, he left many sketches made from nature; it's
possible his paintings were inspired by real-life impressions rather than invented in the
studio. Yet they do have metaphysical content. The fresh foliage on the old sturdy tree
and the peasants bustling around the lopsided shack prompt thoughts of the
continuation of a way of life established over centuries, regardless of daily hardships.

Jan Jozefsz van Goyen. *Winter Scene near The Hague*. 1645. Oil on canvas.
20 ½ x 27 ½ in. (52 x 70 cm).
Despite his strong reputation, van Goyen was unable to provide for his family on an
artist's income. With varying degrees of success, he also traded tulip bulbs, brokered real
estate, and acted as an appraiser for auction houses. Meanwhile his painting evolved,
and he produced his best works in the early 1640s at The Hague. Using lighter
and brighter paints and, most importantly, unifying the view through a general tone in
which the grey-blue hues of sky and water predominate, van Goyen conveys well
Holland's distinctive maritime atmosphere.

Aert van der Neer. *Landscape with a Windmill*. Ca. 1646. Oil on panel. 27 ⅛ x 36 ¼ in. (69 x 92 cm).
Van der Neer enriched the tonal landscape, one of the outstanding achievements of 17th-century Dutch painting, with moonlit and, less often, sunset views. Without pursuing monumentality or outpourings of emotion, he achieved great mastery in conveying nuances of lighting. In the 19th century he was rated highly by both the pioneers of Realist landscape and the German Romantics, one of whom—Philipp Otto Runge—believed that, for his own genre, van der Neer was no less significant than Raphael.

Jacob Isaacksz van Ruisdael. *Seashore*.
Late 1660s–early 1670s. Oil on canvas.
20 ½ x 26 ¾ in. (52 x 68 cm).
Ruisdael's sea is usually neither
spectacularly stormy nor peaceful, as in
the works of many of his contemporary
seascape painters, who depicted it as an
extension of a Dutch town. In fact, he
depicts the determining component of
his country's atmosphere: the wind that
constantly stirs up waves and agitates
clouds in the boundless sky. By eschewing
excessively thorough detail, he sometimes
manages to convey a fleeting impression,
extending a hand to the pioneers of 19th-
century French plein-air painting, such as
Boudin and Daubigny.

BELOW

Jacob Isaacksz van Ruisdael. *Waterfall in Norway*. Late 1660s–early 1670s.
Oil on canvas. 42 ½ x 56 in. (108 x 142.5 cm).
Ruisdael never visited Scandinavia, but he borrowed the idea of Norwegian
landscapes from Allaert van Everdingen, an artist who worked for a time
in Haarlem and had success with such works. A rush of water carrying away a broken
tree, a house huddled on a slope, and tiny figures beneath a clouded sky—all these
components make it possible to see the painting as a piece of 17th-century
speculation on the romantic opposition of man and the elements.

Jacob Isaacksz van Ruisdael. *The Marsh*. 1660s. Oil on canvas. 28 ½ x 39 in.
(72.5 x 99 cm).
Ruisdael, the most outstanding landscape artist of the Dutch golden age, grew up in
Haarlem in the milieu of the genre's best exponents. In Amsterdam in the 1660s he
reached his peak, giving full rein to the tendency to seek out monumental forms and
epic content in the world around him. These huge old trees, ready to tumble into
muddy waters below, come across as a metaphor for all-powerful death that, although
scary, is an implacable law of nature.

LEFT

Paulus Potter. *The Farm*. 1649. Oil on
canvas. 31 ⅞ x 45 ½ in. (81 x 115.5 cm).
The Farm acquired a certain notoriety
due to its extreme naturalism in the
depiction of domestic animals. Nowadays
it is impossible not to notice the overlap
between the coarse materiality that
combines strangely with a delicate
painting technique in Potter's work and
the famous scene at the agricultural show
in Flaubert's novel *Madame Bovary*,
in which the banal presentation of awards
to the breeders is similarly intercut with
the ardent speeches of the seducer.

COVTE ISRAEL.
I
E SVIS LE SEIGNR
ON DIEV, QVI T'AY
TIRE DE LA TERRE
D'EGIPTE DE LA MAISON
DE SERVITVDE. TV
N'AVRAS POINT D'AV-
TRES DIEVX DEVANT
MA FACE. TV NE TE
FERAS POINT D'IDOLE
NI D'IMAGE TAILLEE
NY AVCVNE FIGVRE
POVR LES ADORER.
II
TV NE PRANDRAS POINT
LE NOM DV SEIGNEVR
TON DIEV EN VAIN; CAR
LE SEIGNEVR TON DI-
EV NE TIENDRA PO-
INT POVR INNOCENT
CELVY QVI AVRA PRIS
LE NOM DV SEIGNEVR
SON DIEV EN VAIN.
III
SOVVIENS-TOY DE
SANCTIFIER LE IOVR
DV SABATH.
IV
HONORE TON PERE ET
TA MERE, AFIN QVE T
SOIS HVREVX, ET QV
TV VIVES LOG. TEM
SVR LA TERRE.
V
TV NE TVERAS POINT
VI
TV NE COMMETTRAS
POINT FORNICATION.
VII
TV NE DEROBERAS
POINT.
VIII
TV NE DIRAS POINT
FAVX TESMOIGNAG
CONTRE TON PROCH
AIN
IX
TV NE DESIRERAS
POINT LA FEMME DE
TON PROCHAIN.
X
TV NE DESIRERAS
POINT SA MAISON. N
SON SERVITEVR. N
SA SERVANTE, NY S
BOEVF, NY SON A
NY AVTRE
LVY APP

OPPOSITE
Philippe de Champaigne. *Moses with the Ten Commandments*. 1648. Oil on canvas.
36 x 29 ⅜ in. (91.5 x 74.5 cm).
In the early 1640s, after his son's sudden death, the court painter Philippe de
Champaigne produced a series for the abbey of Port-Royal, thus beginning his flowering
as a religious painter. In portraits and biblical scenes produced over the next 20 years, he
accentuated the moral content and spiritual passion of his subjects. These aspects are
already evident in this work, in which as much attention is devoted to the tablets bearing
the Ten Commandments as to the prophet.

ABOVE
Louis Le Nain. *The Milkmaid's Family*. 1640s. Oil on canvas. 20 x 23 ¼ in. (51 x 59 cm).
Unlike in contemporary Dutch genre painting, Le Nain's compositions indicate neither
peasant labors and leisure nor the common people's hard lot. Indeed, the expensive
copper churn and clothing evoke prosperity. This family is more a symbolic expression of
the unity between the inhabitants of central France and their native land. The contrived
combination of a monumental group standing on a hillock as if on a pedestal, with a
majestic panoramic view unfolding behind, has a certain elevated pomp.

RIGHT

Louis Le Nain. *Visit to Grandmother.*
Ca. 1645–48. Oil on canvas.
22 ⅞ x 28 ¾ in. (58 x 73 cm).

Louis Le Nain was one of three painter
brothers who worked together, mainly
on commissions from the Parisian
aristocracy; in the 1640s they turned
their hand to peasant scenes that had
then come in fashion. Devoid of
technical luster, their interiors are
striking for the interweaving of several
melodic threads: approaching and
retreating figures, illuminated and shady
areas, and the glances the personages
seem to give each other before turning a
common hospitable gaze to the viewer
and the world.

ABOVE

Jacques Bellange. *The Lamentation*. 1615–16. Oil on canvas. 45 ¼ x 69 in.
(115 x 175 cm).

This *Lamentation*—one of the few surviving paintings by Bellange, an artist and
engraver who worked at the court of dukes Charles III and Henry II of Lorraine—is a
rare example of French Mannerism in religious art. The fanciful interlacing of zigzag
lines and the sharp contrasts of light and shade intensify the sense of mental anguish
evident even in the face of the donor, on the right (perhaps a portrait of Bellange's
ducal patron).

OPPOSITE

Pierre Mignard. *The Mystic Marriage of St. Catherine*. 1669. Oil on canvas.
52 ¾ x 41 ⅜ in. (134 x 105 cm).

Despite its title, this painting, by one of the two greatest French decorative painters of
Louis XIV's time (the other was Charles Le Brun), has nothing mystic about it. The
appearance of the Virgin Mary to the holy martyr with the Christ Child, who places a
ring on the girl's finger to confirm her union with her "heavenly bridegroom," is
presented as an idyllic genre scene.

Nicolas Poussin. *The Battle of the Israelites and Amelikites*. 1624–25. Oil on canvas. 38 ⅜ x 52 ¾ in. (97.5 x 134 cm). Poussin's paintings display a highly idiosyncratic French rationalism. Already in this early work, one of the first painted after his arrival in Italy, he places two radically distinct subjects—the "thick of the battle" and Moses praying (which ultimately decides the outcome)—into a tight picture space, distorting proportions but, in exchange, achieving unity and extreme intensity of action.

Luca Giordano. *Battle between the Lapiths and the Centaurs*. 1688. Oil on canvas. 100 ⅜ x 153 ½ in. (255 x 390 cm). The conflict between the Lapiths, a semimythical tribe of giants, and the Centaurs is supposed to have broken out at their king's wedding, when the Centaurs tried to abduct the bride. Giordano persuasively presents the details while demonstrating the breadth of his abilities. In the foreground, passions rage and threaten to spill off the canvas as the delightful natural wealth in the landscape recalls the happy celebration so rudely interrupted.

Nicolas Poussin. *Tancred and Erminia*. Late 1620s–early 1630s. Oil on canvas. 38 ½ x 57 ⅝ in. (98. 5 x 146.5 cm). This painting illustrates a key moment in Torquato Tasso's poem *Jerusalem Delivered*, when Erminia, the daughter of the king of Antioch, uses the magical power of her hair to save her wounded sweetheart, the crusader Tancred. Poussin demonstrates his ability to moderate passions while presenting an enchanting balance of influences. Neither anatomical precision, nor the eloquence of gestures, nor the power of bright patches of color becomes an end in itself, but together they produce a formula of love and duty that we read without being distracted by superfluous effects.

Nicolas Poussin. *Landscape with Polyphemus*. 1649. Oil on canvas. 59 x 78 ⅜ in. (150 x 199 cm). Poussin's landscapes are striking for his indifference to the illusion of boundless distance, although he perfectly mastered the techniques used to produce it. He requires only a small theatrical space to allow our eye to delve into and assess the scale of the blooming valley and the mountains, to notice the enormous Cyclops playing his pipes beneath the sky, and even to enjoy his music, which swells toward the foreground in colors that grow ever more intense, attaining clarity in the group of nature deities at the painting's edge.

OPPOSITE, TOP

Claude Gellée, called Le Lorrain. *Landscape with Apollo and the Cumaean Sibyl*. Between 1645 and 1649.
Oil on canvas. 39 ⅛ x 50 in. (99.5 x 127 cm).

In Ovid's *Metamorphoses* the Cumaean sibyl recounts how Apollo, trying to gain her love, offered anything her heart desired. So, forgetting how quickly youth passes, she picked up a handful of sand and asked the god to give her as many days as there were grains of sand in her palm. Lorrain sets this melancholic subject among overgrown ancient ruins. Thus, after thoughts of the perishability of human beings and their creations, the viewer can find consolation in contemplating the happy eternity of nature.

OPPOSITE, BOTTOM

Claude Gellée, called Le Lorrain. *Landscape with Jacob Wrestling with the Angel*. 1672. Oil on canvas.
44 ½ x 61 ⅞ in. (113 x 157 cm).

On returning to Canaan, Jacob, who feared his elder brother Esau's vengeance, sent his servants ahead with a peace offering. That night an angel came to him, and they wrestled until daybreak. By remaining undefeated, Jacob earned God's blessing and a new name, Israel. Lorrain incorporated this subject into one of his few night scenes, linking the first rays of the morning sun with the favorable outcome of this turning point in the biblical story.

ABOVE

Claude Gellée, called Le Lorrain. *Morning (Landscape with Jacob and Rachel at the Well)*. 1666. Oil on canvas.
44 ½ x 61 ⅞ in. (113 x 157 cm).

Although the majority of Lorrain's landscapes incorporated biblical, mythological, or genre scenes, his main theme was transformations of light; indeed, many of his series are devoted to times of day. Nature was his passion, as demonstrated not only by his superb sketches made on location but also by his practice, highly unusual for the 17th century, of mixing paints while watching a sunrise or sunset, to be used later in the studio.

RIGHT

Charles-Antoine Coypel. *The Fury of Achilles*. 1737. Oil on canvas. 57 ⅞ x 76 ¾ in. (147 × 195 cm).

Coypel had an excellent knowledge of ancient literature and here he precisely illustrated a passage from Homer's *Iliad*: Poseidon and Athena, having assumed human form, support the hero Achilles as he rushes at the Trojans. In the foreground are the river god Scamander (Xanthos) and his brother Simoeis, also sworn enemies of Achilles, while in the sky Hephaestus, carrying torches, is rushing to his aid, sent by the goddess Hera.

Antoine Watteau. *Actors of the Comédie-Française.* Ca. 1712. Oil on panel.
7 ⅞ x 9 ⅞ in. (20 x 25 cm).
This tiny composition, the earliest of the Hermitage's paintings by Watteau, consists of
four virtuoso portraits displaying both character and vivid immediacy. Only the head of
the young black boy is a stock image, like the roles he probably performed on stage. The
dense painting contains a multitude of shades applied with small fastidious brushstrokes
and is no less rich in color than the artist's gallant scenes set in the open air.

Antoine Watteau. *Savoyard with a Marmot.* 1716. Oil on canvas.
16 x 12 ¾ in. (40.5 x 32.5 cm).
Everything here is archaic: the peasant type posing awkwardly in the center has its
origins in 17th-century engravings; the landscape seems completely separate, like a
theatrical backdrop. But in Watteau's hands these vestiges of the past become a
retrospective view that is not only touching but also intelligent. Even the timidity
evident in the molding of the figure works to the benefit of the stylization.

ABOVE

Antoine Watteau. *An Embarrassing Proposal*. Ca. 1716. Oil on canvas. 25 ½ x 33 ¼ in. (65 x 84.5 cm).

One of the gallant scenes in which Watteau precisely captured the 18th-century's theatricalized view of the world shows not a stage production but people dressed and behaving in a theatrical manner, perceiving the world and themselves as a performance. Watteau registers the unstable boundary between reality and the conception of it; most important here is the atmosphere, the figures dissolved in the landscape, the general haze of colors, in which the shades of sky, foliage, and expensive fabrics coexist on equal terms.

Antoine Watteau. *A Capricious Woman* ("La Boudeuse"). Ca. 1718. Oil on canvas. 16 ½ x 13 ⅜ in. (42 x 34 cm).

The close-up view reveals the artificiality of Watteau's world but only enhances its charm. The smooth carpet of the lawn, the trees with twisted trunks, and the little leaves each painted separately call to mind "Le Douanier" Rousseau. Yet, the extremely fine painting of the faces and the tangible shifting of the silk nervously crumpled in the heroine's hand prompt the suspicion that Watteau deliberately used the naïveté of the landscape to echo the childish distress of a little girl in a woman's body.

OPPOSITE
François Le Moyne. *Female Bather*. Mid-1720s. Oil on canvas. 54 ⅜ x 42 in. (138 x 106.5 cm).
Le Moyne created this painting during his time in Venice and Rome, and the sculptural molding of the figures
and the drapes painted with bright local colors show the Italian influence. Yet the carefree eroticism, which no longer
needs the justification of a mythological or biblical subject, and attention to fleeting bodily sensations make this work
a typical example of the French Rococo.

ABOVE
Nicolas Lancret. *Portrait of the Dancer Camargo*. Ca. 1732. Oil on canvas. 17 ¾ x 21 ⅝ in. (45 x 55 cm).
Lancret, a pupil of Antoine Watteau, displays a more appreciable Dutch influence, reflecting the shift in tastes among
collectors and artists in the early 18th century. The work is also a composite of predictable elements: a Franco-Dutch
idyllic landscape, a sumptuous dress taken from formal portraits, and a handful of musicians in the Rococo tradition.
Stylization can hardly explain the ungainly pose of the famous Marie-Anne Camargo (1710–70), who introduced into
female ballet the rapid unrestrained movements previously used only by men.

RIGHT

Giovanni Battista Tiepolo. *Maecenas Presenting the Liberal Arts to Augustus.* 1743. Oil on canvas. 27 ⅜ x 35 in. (69.5 x 89 cm).

This painting was originally a gift to the major collector Heinrich Brühl, the powerful prime minister of Elector Frederick Augustus II of Saxony, also King Augustus III of Poland. It came into the Hermitage when Catherine II purchased Brühl's entire collection early in the museum's history. In presenting an ancient example of patronage of the arts, Tiepolo was extolling one of the characteristics of an enlightened monarchy, which the Russian empress was also seeking to establish.

François Boucher. *Pastoral Scene*. 1740s.
Oil on canvas. 24 x 29 ½ in.
(61 x 75 cm) oval.
In Boucher's ingenuous pastoral scenes, the desire to please—which in combination with a predilection for captivating subjects and monumental theatrics would lead to the decline of 19th-century academic Neoclassicism—enchants us, just as it did Diderot and his contemporaries, with its pure aestheticism.

François Boucher. *Landscape near Beauvais*. Early 1740s. Oil on canvas. 19 ¼ x 22 ⅞ in. (49 x 58 cm).
In the same way that nudity was finally emancipated in Rococo art (in Boucher's oeuvre, courtesans are seen basking in bed),
landscape rid itself of the last vestiges of narrative. Born of the artist's imagination and deriving conflict-free unity from this, the scene
nonetheless consists entirely of details, including the girl calmly doing the laundry, the thoughtful boy next to her, and the doves
fluttering above the roof of the cottage.

ABOVE
Alessandro Magnasco. *Banditti at Rest*. 1710s. Oil on canvas. 44 x 63 ¾ in. (112 x 162 cm).
The atmosphere of a mysterious theatrical action, full of allusions and understatements, links Magnasco's painting to the work of
Watteau, his contemporary. On Italian soil, however, the performance takes place amid different scenery. In place of the rural idyll are
ancient ruins, turned from an object of admiration into a source of amusement. And instead of languorous ladies and ceremonious
gentlemen there are absurd little figures painted with a few touches of the brush.

P. 292 TOP
Michele Marieschi. *The Rialto Bridge in Venice*. 1740s. Oil on canvas (transferred from panel). 51 ⅛ x 77 in. (130 x 195.5 cm).
With Canaletto and Guardi, Marieschi was one of the leading exponents of the Venetian *veduta*, a highly detailed urban landscape
that became fashionable with aristocrats, mainly Englishmen, touring Italy in ever-increasing numbers. The covered Rialto Bridge took
its name from a nearby market. Merchants' shops were built on it in the 15th century, and until the 19th century it was the only bridge
over the Grand Canal, linking the two central parts of the city.

OPPOSITE, BOTTOM
Antonio Canal, called Canaletto. *The Reception of the French Ambassador in Venice*. 1726/27. Oil on canvas.
71 ¼ x 102 ⅛ in. (181 x 259.5 cm).
If we compare this painting by Canaletto with the depictions of official occasions produced by Carpaccio and Gentile
Bellini, we immediately notice how much smaller the human figures are, making it no easy matter to single out the two
main protagonists: Count Languet de Gergy, the French ambassador, and the Venetian Doge. Venice's economic might
was a thing of the past, and the artist is now far more interested in the city's buildings and the soft light bathing them.

ABOVE
Francesco Guardi. *View of a Square and Palace*. Between 1775 and 1780. Oil on canvas (transferred from panel).
10 ⅝ x 9 in. (27 x 23 cm).
Along with collecting *vedute*, visitors to Venice liked to buy imaginary landscapes known as *capriccios*. Some works
unite architectural elements from different parts of the city; others, like Guardi's, show an arbitrary corner, devoting far
more attention to atmosphere and the play of light and color than to the buildings and people's daily lives. The places
he depicted are often unidentifiable, but his works are not intellectual curiosities. They appeal more to emotions, and
in them Venice first acquired the romantic charm of decay.

Pietro Longhi. *A Theatrical Scene*. Ca. 1752. Oil on canvas. 24 ½ x 19 ⅝ in. (62 x 50 cm).
Longhi's amusing genre scenes allow us to form an impression of the fashion, habits, and
general half-real, half-fantastic atmosphere of 18th-century Venice, which had lost its
political might and turned into a city of amusements, spectacles, and gambling. The
painting's plot is unclear, but it is obviously a risqué love scene from an Italian comedy
featuring a fat doctor (or notary) and the servant girl Columbine.

Jean-Marc Nattier. *Portrait of a Lady in Grey*. Early 18th century. Oil on canvas. 31 ½ x 25 ⅛ in. (80 x 64 cm) oval.
This fashionable early-18th-century portraitist caught Peter the Great's attention in 1717, when he was visiting
The Hague with his wife, Empress Catherine. Nattier painted both of them and, according to his daughter's
memoirs, received an invitation to Russia, which he declined. This splendid example of his graceful style
may depict another exalted personage—Louise-Adélaïde, Duchess of Orleans, a daughter of the French regent.

Rembrandt f
1639

Western European Graphic Arts, 15th–Early 18th Century

Andrea Mantegna. *Madonna and Child.* Ca. 1490–91. Engraving. 8 ½ x 7 ½ in. (21.7 x 18.9 cm).
Although in his biography of Mantegna, Giorgio Vasari states that the artist was the first in Italy to master the technique of copper engraving, scholars differ on whether Mantegna did the engravings himself or supplied drawings to professional printmakers. The print specialist David Landau counts this work among the best done by the master. A Mantegna painting with a similar composition, in Padua's Eremitani Museum, may have served as the basis for this print.

François Clouet. *Portrait of Charles IX.* 1560s. Deux crayons (sanguine and black chalk).
13 ⅛ x 8 ⅞ in. (33.5 x 22.5 cm).
Judging by the fact that in 1571 Clouet was summoned to the Mint in Paris to assess how well the image on a coin resembled the monarch, his portraits of Charles IX (r. 1563–74) were considered exemplary. This drawing was made in preparation for a portrait now in the Hôtel d'Assézat, in Toulouse. It shows the king as a young man, a few years before the infamous St. Bartholomew's Day Massacre (August 24/25, 1572), which was the chief event of his reign.

1566.

1569

le roi Charles IX

ABOVE

Francesco Mazzola, known as Parmigianino. *Lovers*. Ca. 1528. Etching, with engraving and dry-point. 5 x 4 in. (14.7 x 10.3 cm).

Parmigianino was one of the first in Italy to try etching and found the medium well suited to his impetuous temperament. A fine stroke, permitting far more nuances than in a pencil drawing, becomes in this example the conductor of the excitement possessing not just the couple who have secluded themselves in a wood but the entire natural setting, which is treated in an almost expressionistic manner.

RIGHT

Annibale Carracci. *The Pieta Caprarola*. 1597. Etching, with engraving and dry-point. 4 ⅞ x 6 ¼ in. (12.3 x 16 cm).

Carracci was a master of eloquent composition, a virtuoso who easily made the transition from sublime harmony to naturalism. Here he uses etching as a means of dramatization. Because it was executed with engraving tools, his drawing, usually light and economical, renders the figures' contours sharp and abstract. The puffs of smoke in the background, apparently due to insufficient masking during the etching process, heighten the scene's emotional tension.

1507.   Nico Van Aelst for.

1523
L

LEFT
Lucas van Leyden. *The Tooth-Puller*.
1523. Engraving. 5 ⅞ x 3 ¾ in.
(14.9 x 9.6 cm).
"He lies like a tooth-puller" is an old
French saying, and the fairground dentist
depicted here does indeed know how
to sell himself: trophy teeth adorning his
beret, a diploma with a wax seal,
instruments carefully laid out, a self-
possessed appearance—all bring him
a good income, judging by his expensive
clothing. This engraving by Lucas van
Leyden, a pioneer of Dutch genre
painting, served as a prototype for many
painted versions.

OPPOSITE
Albrecht Dürer. *Melancholia I*. 1513.
Burin engraving. 9 ⅝ x 7 ⅜ in.
(24.4 x 18.7 cm).
For Dürer, art became a tool of self-
knowledge on a par with science.
Numbering himself among the
melancholics—who have a black humor
that balances between depression and
enthusiasm but inclines to deep thought
and insight—he assembles here a host of
symbols associated with melancholia.
Some (the scales, the star) allude to an
apocalyptic foreboding; others (the
compasses, magic square, polyhedron)
point to scientific activities; still more
(the pensive angel, hound, ladder,
hourglass) to both. Together they present
a picture of expectation of doomsday as
well as the pursuit of saving knowledge.

Rembrandt. ƒ:. 1638.

Rembrandt Harmensz. van Rijn. *Adam and Eve*. 1638. Etching; 2nd state of 2. 6 ½ x 4 ½ in. (16.3 x 11.5 cm).
In contrast to Gospel subjects, which he invested with an air of the miraculous, Rembrandt often treated Old Testament events in a down-to-earth manner, as ordinary episodes from human history. Adam and Eve's naturally imperfect bodies may have been borrowed from the beggars he often sketched in the poor quarters of Leiden. Thus the theme of paradise lost paradoxically—yet with faultless logic—echoes the theme of poverty stripped not of vices, but of the far greater evil of narcissism.

Hendrick Goltzius. *Bacchus, Venus, and Ceres*. 1606. Pencil, pen, and brown wash on grounded canvas. 89 ¾ x 67 in. (228 x 170 cm).
This huge drawing is no sketch for a painting but rather a demonstration of the inimitable skill of a Dutch artist famed in his own lifetime as a magnificent engraver and draughtsman. Cupid hardens his arrows in a fire lit on the altar of love, fuelled by vine leaves and corn cobs—attributes of the deities of wine and fertility without whom, as the Latin poet Terence put it, Venus freezes. Next to him Goltzius depicted himself, wittily likening his engraver's tool to the all-penetrating arrows of love.

Peter Paul Rubens. *Head of a Youth*. Ca. 1615. Charcoal and chalk on grey paper.
13 ⅜ x 10 ⅝ in. (34 x 27 cm).
This preparatory study for a large altarpiece depicting the stoning of St. Stephen
allows us to judge how Rubens reworked ancient models in his own creations. While
creating a mirror image of the sketch he made in the Uffizi Gallery of the Roman bust
The Dying Alexander the Great, the artist stressed the light and dark areas with charcoal
and chalk, investing the work with the naturalness of a sketch made from life and
"animating the marble."

BELOW
Nicolas Poussin. *Baptism*. 1644–45. Black chalk, bister pen and wash.
6 ½ x 10 in. (16.5 x 25.4 cm).
This drawing shows Poussin developing the composition for his painting of the
same name, one of a cycle of *The Seven Sacraments* commissioned by Paul Fréart
de Chantelou, a prominent collector. The artist often made such sketches from wax
figures, which allowed him to achieve maximum accuracy in light and shade. Because
of the elaborate poses and numerous gestures, the scene resembles an intellectual
debate about faith, with a secular character emphasized by the setting of ancient ruins.

Jacques Callot. *The Temptation of St. Anthony.* 1634. Black chalk, bister pen and wash, sanguine, and gouache.
17 ¾ x 26 ⅜ in. (45 x 67 cm).

In less than two decades, Callot progressed from depictions of strange semifantastic figures—theatrical stock characters—to complex large-scale compositions on small etching plates. These sometimes surpass the era's Baroque paintings for epic persuasiveness (the *Miseries of War* cycle) or scope of imagination, as in this *Temptation*, a sketch for an etching of the same name. The image of the tiny saint persecuted by demons may have been inspired by events in the artist's native Lorraine, seized and devastated by the French at this time.

Giovanni Battista Piranesi. *The Round Tower* (sheet 3). 1749/50. From the Prisons series. Etching; 1st state of 6.
21 ⅞ x 16 ½ in. (55.6 x 41.8 cm).

In comparison with the first modern prison designs, which also appeared in the 18th century and sought to achieve total visibility (one of the expressions of the Enlightenment belief in all-powerful reason), Piranesi's imaginary constructions are striking for their irrationality. A keen scholar of ancient architecture, he invests them with fine proportions, yet more convincingly depicts chaos, something that still repelled his contemporaries but would soon become attractive to the Romantics—artists and naturalists.

François Boucher. *Study of a Nude.* 1740. Trois crayons on brown paper.
10 ⅜ x 13 ⅝ in. (26.2 x 34.6 cm).

When nudity became a natural subject in the 18th century, artists began to pursue naturalness in its depiction. And the naturalness of nakedness is of a different kind from that of a pose or facial expression: it demands from the artist not so much a sure hand as sureness of feeling. So Boucher's finest drawings are marked not by the affectation that one might expect from the gallant age, but by lively improvisation.

BELOW

Antoine Watteau. *Study of a Female Head.* 1710s. Trois crayons on light brown paper.
13 x 9 in. (33 x 23 cm).

In his paintings Watteau avoids excessive individualization, preferring vivid character and the nuances of shifting mood over precise features. His drawings leave no doubt that the reason has nothing to do with a lack of firmness in his hand. If he had not discovered an inclination for gallant scenes, with their theatrical volatility, we would certainly have lost the Watteau we know but might possibly have gained a perspicacious portraitist, the like of which 18th-century France never produced.

Western European Sculpture, 15th–Early 18th Century

Gian Lorenzo Bernini. *The Ecstasy of St. Theresa*. 1640s. Terracotta. 18 ½ in. (47 cm) high.

The marble sculptural group that Bernini produced on this subject for the Cornaro chapel in Rome's Church of Santa Maria della Vittoria is the apogee of Baroque sculpture. The "sweet torment" that Theresa of Avila experienced through a vision of an angel piercing her body with a spear found almost literal expression in the combination of the soft treatment of the face and hands and the sharp folds of the clothing that seems to be fluttering in a gust of wind.

Workshop of Andrea della Robbia. *Madonna and Child*. Early 16th century. Majolica. 50 ⅜ in. (128 cm) high.
Color is an inseparable part of the medieval tradition of religious art: the statues in Romanesque and Gothic churches
were painted right up to the 16th century. Florentine sculptures in the majolica technique—earthenware with a colored
glaze introduced by Andrea's uncle Luca della Robbia—combined the charming simplicity and ornamental quality of
folk art with a true-to-life depiction of the human figures.

RIGHT

Hans Klocker. *St. Stephen.* Between 1490 and 1495. Polychrome wood (paint remnants). 38 ⅛ in. (97 cm) high. Gothic sculptors followed the same path—from statue-columns and relief decorations to sculpture in the round—as their ancient forerunners, but their means of conquering space was the expressive line rather than the anatomical softness of volumes. In Northern Europe this evolution can be traced in carved wooden altars, one of which included this piece, from the workshop of a celebrated Austrian sculptor. The first Christian martyr is presented in a deacon's robes holding a prayer book and stones, the instrument of his death.

P. 318

Antonio Rossellino. *The Virgin and Child.* 1460s. Marble. 26 ⅜ x 20 ¼ in. (67 x 51.5 cm).
Donatello, the inventor of the *relieve schiacciato* ("flattened relief") technique, employed it not to take sculpture out into space, as all his contemporaries sought to do, but to depict space within the marble, indicating soil, trees, and clouds with fine surface gradations. His followers, including Rossellino, one of the leading Florentine sculptors of the 1400s, uncovered the decorative potential of this technique. He invested his works with the lightness of a vision, superbly "drawing with the chisel," which led to the technique often becoming known as "painting in relief."

P. 319, ABOVE

Jean Goujon. *Venus and Cupid.* 1540s. Marble. 20 x 22 ⅜ in. (51 x 57 cm) (oval). This relief almost certainly came from the Château d'Anet, one of the outstanding creations of the French Renaissance, built and decorated on King Henry II's orders for his mistress, Diane de Poitiers. A superbly educated beauty, connoisseur, and patron of the arts, Diane played a major role in the formation of a refined artistic school around the court. Besides Goujon, she supported the architect Philibert de l'Orme, the poet Pierre Ronsard, and the painter François Clouet and often acted as a model for the mythological compositions of artists and sculptors.

BELOW

Antonio Lombardo. *Vulcan's Forge.*
Between 1508 and 1516. Marble.
32 ¾ x 41 ¾ in. (83 x 106 cm).
Interest in the legacy of antiquity grew
from the 14th century on, and by the
early 16th century it had become the
foundation of an elite aristocratic culture.
Artists and their patrons had a perfect
command of the language of Greek
philosophy and mythology. The exact
subject of this relief, created by the
Venetian sculptor to adorn the
apartments of Duke Alfonso d'Este of
Ferrara, is not clear. The personage on
the left, in the pose of Laocoön (the
famous sculptural group had just been
discovered in Rome, in 1506), may be
Zeus, from whose head Athena will
emerge, or Prometheus being chained
to a rock by Vulcan for giving fire to
humans.

Michelangelo Buonarroti. *Crouching Boy*. Between 1530 and 1534. Marble. 21 ¼ in. (54 cm) high.

Judging by a surviving drawing, Michelangelo intended this figure for the Medici tombs in Florence's Basilica of San Lorenzo, one of his greatest achievements. The memorial ensemble, conceived as an allegory of the inexorable march of time, was not completed in accordance with the original project. The statue of a boy may have been made for one of the niches in a tomb and may symbolize the awakening soul or, on the contrary, death—all proposed interpretations are disputed.

RIGHT

Baccio Bandinelli (born Bartolommeo Brandini). *Faun*. 1540s. Marble. 22 ⅞ in. (58 cm) high.

The talents of Baccio Bandinelli— an ambitious imitator and rival of Michelangelo, who found success at the court of Cosimo I Medici—revealed themselves particularly in drawing and small-scale plastic art. His monumental sculptural groups are full of contradictions and compositional discord, but in his smaller works he demonstrates the clear molding of volumes, smooth treatment of the marble, and moderate use of detail that laid the foundation for academic Classicism.

Giuseppe Mazzuola. *The Death of Adonis*. 1709. Marble.
76 in. (193 cm) high.
The exceptional beauty of this child, the fruit of an incestuous union engineered by the insulted Aphrodite, caused an argument among the gods that could only end in his death: he was killed by a boar while hunting. In devoting one of his chief works to that fatal incident, Mazzuola expressed in a typically Baroque depiction of a dramatic moment the idea of the transience of beauty.

François Girardon. *Model for an Equestrian Statue of Louis XIV*. 1680s–90s. Bronze.
40 ½ in. (103 cm) high.
This sculpture was commissioned in 1685 to adorn the Place Vendôme in Paris. Taking as his prototype the monument to Marcus Aurelius in Rome , Girardon depicted the king as a triumphant general astride a horse without a saddle or stirrups, in ancient dress but with the wig characteristic of his own time. The monument, 17 meters (56 ft.) high with the pedestal, was destroyed during the French Revolution and is known today by only a few scale models.

Selected Bibliography

Alekseyev, A. Yu., V. Yu. Murzin, and R. Rolle. *Chertomlyk (Skifsky tsarsky kurgan IV v. do n.e.)*. Kiev: 1991.

Arsinoya ili Kleopatra?, Exhibition catalogue compiled by A. Bolshakov, O. Neverov, and Yu. Diukov. St. Petersburg: 2002.

Artamonov, M. I. *Sokrovishcha skifskikh kurganov v sobranii Gosudarstvennogo Ermitazha*. Prague and Leningrad: 1966.

Baddeley, Oriana, Earleen Brunner, Marlia Mundell Mango, and Yuri Piatnitsky, eds. *Sinai, Byzantium, Russia. Orthodox Art from the Sixth to the Twentieth Century*, Exhibition catalogue. St. Petersburg and London: 2000.

Baticle, Jeannine, ed. *Zurbarán*. New York: The Metropolitan Museum of Art, 1987.

Benua [Benois], A. *Putevoditel po kertinnoi geleree Imperatorskogo Ermitazha*. St. Petersburg: Publication of the Society of St. Eugenia, 1910.

Brown, Christopher. *Scenes of Everyday Life. Dutch Genre Painting of the Seventeenth Century*. London: Faber and Faber, 1984.

Clark, Kenneth. *Landscape into Art*. London: John Murray, 1949.

Daniel, S. M. *Rembrandt* [in Russian]. St. Petersburg: Aurora Art Publishers, 2002.

———. *Rokoko. Ot Vatto do Fragonara*. St. Petersburg: Azbuka-Klassika, 2007.

Descargues, Pierre. *Le Musée de l'Ermitage*. Paris: Editions Aimery Somogy, 1961.

Fomitchova, Tatyana D., ed. *Venetian Painting: Fourteenth to Eighteenth Centuries (The Hermitage catalogue of Western European painting)*. Milano: Giunti Gruppo Editoriale, 1993.

Gold der Skythen: Schätze aus der Staatlichen Eremitage. St. Petersburg, Hamburg: 1993.

Gorbunova, K. S. *Chernofigurnye atticheskiye vazy v Ermitazhe: Katalog cobraniya*. Leningrad: 1983.

Haak, Bob. *The Golden Age. Dutch Painters of the Seventeenth Century*. London: Thames and Hudson, 1984.

———. *Rembrandt: His Life, His Work, His Time*. New York: Harry N. Abrams, Inc., 1969.

Hartt, Frederick. *History of Italian Renaissance Art. Painting, Sculpture, Architecture*, 3rd edition. New York: Harry N. Abrams Inc., 1987.

Iran v Ermitazhe. Formirovaniye kollektsii, Exhibition catalogue written and compiled by A. T. Adamova and A. B. Nikitin. St. Petersburg: 2004.

Kagane Ludmila, Albert Kostenevitch, eds. *Spanish Painting: Fifteenth to Eighteenth Centuries (The Hermitage catalogue of Western European painting)*. Milano: Giunti Gruppo Editoriale, 1997.

Kalashnik, Yuri. *Greek Gold from the Treasure Rooms of the Hermitage*. Exhibition catalogue. Amsterdam: 2004.

Kostsova, A. S. *Drevnerusskaya zhivopis v sobranii Ermitazha*. St. Petersburg: 1992.

Krasnofigurnye atticheskiye vazy v Ermitazhe: Katalog cobraniya, compiled by A. A. Peredolskaya. Leningrad: 1967.

Kustodieva, Tatyana K., ed. *Italian Painting: Thirteenth to Sixteenth Centuries (The Hermitage catalogue of Western European painting)*. Milano: Giunti Gruppo Editoriale, 1994.

Kuznetsov, Yuri. *Risunki Rubensa*. Moscow: Iskusstvo, 1974.

———, ed. *The Hermitage. Western European Drawing*. Leningrad: Aurora Art Publishers, 1981.

Landa, N., and I. Lapis. *Egyptian Antiquities in the Hermitage*. Leningrad: 1974.

Lapis, I. A., and M. E. Matye. *Drevneegipetskaya skulptura v sobranii Gosudarstvennogo Ermitazha*. Moscow: 1969.

Lapkovskaya, E. A. *Prikladnoye iskusstvo srednikh vekov v Gosudarstvennov Ermitazhe*. Moscow: Iskusstvo, 1971.

Levey, Michael. *Rococo to Revolution: Major Trends in Eighteenth Century Painting*. London: Thames and Hudson, 1966.

Levinson-Lessing, V. F. *Istoriya kartinnoi galerei Ermitazha*. Leningrad: Iskusstvo, 1986.

Loukonine, V., and A. Ivanov. *L'art persan*. Bournemouth, St. Petersburg: 1995.

Lukonin, V. G. *Iskusstvo Drevnogo Irana*. Moscow: 1977.

Malraux, André. *Œuvres complètes IV: Ecrits sur l'art*, Tome I. Paris: Gallimard, Bibliothèque de la Pléiade, 2004.

Marshak, B. I. *Sogdiiskoye serebro. Ocherki po vostochnoi torevtike*. Moscow: 1971.

Nemilova, Inna S., ed. *French Painting: Eighteenth Century (The Hermitage catalogue of Western European painting)*. Milano: Giunti Gruppo Editoriale, 1986.

Nekrasova, Ye. N. *Lazur i zoloto Limozha: email XII–XIV vekov*. St. Petersburg: State Hermitage Publishing House, 2009.

Newerov, Oleg. *Antike Kameen*. Leipzig: 1981.

———. *Great Private Collections of Imperial Russia*. New York: The Vendome Press, 2004.

———. *Kameya Gonzaga. Iz istorii gliptiki*. Leningrad: Aurora Art Publishers, 1977.

Nikulin, Nicolas N. *Zolotoi vek niderlandskoi zhivopisi. XV vek*. Moscow: Izobrazitelnoye Iskusstvo, 1981.

———, ed. *German and Austrian Painting: Fifteenth to Eighteenth Centuries (The Hermitage catalogue of Western European painting)*. Milano: Giunti Gruppo Editoriale, 1987.

———, ed. *Netherlandish Painting: Fifteenth and Sixteenth Centuries (The Hermitage catalogue of Western European painting)*. Milano: Giunti Gruppo Editoriale, 1989.

La peinture française, sous la direction de Jean-Louis Pradel. Paris: Le Robert, 1983.

Piotrovsky, B. B. *Ermitazh. Istoriya i kollektsii*, foreword by Giulio Carlo Argan. Leningrad: Iskusstvo, 1981.

Piotrovsky, B., L. Galanina, and N. Grach. *Scythian Art: The Legacy of the Scythian World: Mid-7th to 3rd century B.C.* Leningrad: 1986.

Letters of Reiner Maria Rilke (1892–1910), translated by Jane Bannard Greene and Norton Herter. New York: W. W. Norton and Company, Inc., 1969.

The Road to Byzantium. Luxury Arts of Antiquity. Exhibition catalogue. London: 2006.

Rolle, R., V. Murzin, and A. Alekseev. "Königskurgan Chertomlyk. Ein skythisher Grabhügel des 4. Jh. v. Chr.," *Hamburger Forschungen zur Archäologie*. Bd 1. 1997. Mainz: 1998.

Samosiuk, K. F. *Buddiiskaya zhivopis iz Khara Khoto. XII–XIV veka*. St. Petersburg: State Hermitage Publishing House, 2006.

Saverkina, I. I. *Grecheskaya skulptura V v. do n.e. v sobranii Ermitazha. Originaly i rimskiye kopii*. Leningrad: 1986.

Sokolova, T. M. *Zdaniya i zaly Ermitazha*. Leningrad: Iskusstvo, 1982.

Sterling, Charles. *Great French Painting in the Hermitage*. New York: Harry N. Abrams, Inc., 1958.

Sutton, Peter C. *Pieter de Hoogh*. London: Phaidon Press, 1980.

Tarasov, Yu. A. *Gollandsky peizazh XVII veka*. Moscow: Izobrazitelnoye Iskusstvo, 1983.

Tout l'œuvre peint de Greco, introduction par Paul Guinard. Paris: Flammarion, 1971.

Trever, K. V. *Pamiatniki greko-baktriiskogo iskusstvf*. Moscow and Leningrad: 1940.

Trofimova, Anna, ed. *Greeks on the Black Sea. Ancient Art from the Hermitage*. Catalogue. Los Angeles: Getty Publications, 2007.

Varshavskaya, Maria, and Xenia Egorova, eds. *Rubens: Paintings from Soviet Museums*. Leningrad: Aurora Art Publishers, 1989.

Verizhnikova, T. F. *Malye gollandtsy*. St. Petersburg: Aurora Art Publishers, 2004.

Vipper, B. R. *Italyanasky Renessans. XIII–XVI veka*, 2 vols. Moscow: Iskusstvo, 1977.

Vostchinina, A. *Musée de l'Ermitage. Le portrait Romain: Album et catalogue illustré de toute la collection*. Leningrad: Aurora Art Publishers, 1974.

Williams, D., and J. Ogden. *Greek Gold: Jewellery of the Classical World*. Exhibition catalogue. London: 1994.

Zwei Gesichter der Eremitage. Scythen und ihr Gold, Bd I: Die Grossen Sammlungen VI. Katalog der Ausstellung. Bonn: 1997.

Credits

Index